FILM INDUSTRIES
IN LATIN AMERICA

COMMUNICATION AND INFORMATION SCIENCE

A series of monographs, treatises, and texts
Edited by
MELVIN J. VOIGT
University of California, San Diego

FILM INDUSTRIES IN LATIN AMERICA: DEPENDENCY AND DEVELOPMENT

Jorge A. Schnitman

ABLEX Publishing Corporation
Norwood, New Jersey 07648

Printed in the United States of America.

Library of Congress Cataloging in Publication Data

Schnitman, Jorge.
    Film industries in Latin America.

    Includes index.
    1. Moving-picture industry—Latin America. 2. Latin America—
Dependency on foreign countries. I. Title.
PN1993.5.L3S27 1983   384'.8'098   83-12244
ISBN 0-89391-095-3

Ablex Publishing Corporation
355 Chestnut Street
Norwood, New Jersey 07648

Contents

Acknowledgements

I would like to acknowledge the Center for Latin American Studies, Stanford University, for providing a warm and stimulating environment for the writing of this book. Special thanks are due to the Center Director, Prof. John Wirth, and to Kathleen F. Durham, Program Coordinator. I am also very grateful to Dr. Dain Borges (Stanford University) and Prof. Randal Johnson (University of Florida) who read the manuscript in its entirety and made many useful comments and suggestions. Prof. Johnson's suggestions on Chapter 5 are specifically acknowledged. As always, my wife and parents supported me well beyond the call of family ties. This book is also theirs.

Chapter 1
Film Industries in Latin America: An Overview

Film is a complex social institution that can be studied from various disciplines and points of view (Metz 1975, 1979). Similar to other social institutions, film industries' modes of production, distribution, and consumption are "overdetermined" phenomena, simultaneously determined by a variety of structural and situational factors. For analytical purposes, however, the factors affecting the growth of national film industries in Latin America can be divided into economic, political, and cultural-ideological. In practice, all the variables identified in this book interact in complex patterns, sometimes complementing and sometimes contradicting each other. The net result has been the enormous difficulties in the historical growth and development of most national film industries in Latin America.

ECONOMIC ASPECTS

It is customary to divide film industries into production, distribution, and exhibition sectors. Production firms manufacture the actual product, which is then handled on a wholesale basis by distribution facilities, and, in turn, is rented to exhibitors who bring the product to the final consumers, the viewers. In capitalist economies, these companies operate under constraints imposed by competition and profit, although they often are able to create a more predictable environment, which allows them to maximize profits and minimize the undesirable effects of competition. This is the function of horizontal and vertical integration. (See page 13.) Although historically, only U.S.-based and some European companies were able to organize and maintain an early vertical integration that made possible the vast accumulation of financial and managerial resources necessary to expand internationally, only U.S.-based companies succeeded in maintaining such distribution networks on a continuing basis. In Latin America, there have been some brief periods of vertical integration of film activities under the control of local capital, and more prolonged experiences under the hegemony of the state. (See Chapters 4 and 5 for examples of variable degrees of vertical integration under state hegemony in Mexico and Brazil.)

Film as a form of entertainment appeared in Latin American soon after the brothers Lumière organized their first show of the new medium in Paris in December 1895. The first Latin American film projections took place in Brazil in July 1896, and in September of the same year in Argentina. However, film came to other Latin American countries much later for example, to Bolivia in 1909. Exhibition facilities developed rapidly throughout Latin America, attracting enthusiastic and predominantly working-class audiences (Chanan, 1976, p. 17). Opera and the legitimate theatre were preferred by the upper classes (Ossa Coo, 1971, p. 11).

Latin American film markets were created originally through European and American products. The market was favorable to U.S. films immediately after the beginning of World War I when, lacking European movies, Latin American distributors and exhibitors turned to Hollywood. By 1916, American silent features dominated Latin American screens. The new medium's business potential increased when distribution switched from selling copies to exhibitors to renting them for a percentage of the gross. This transition and the general growth of the exhibition market favored the policy of the large U.S. companies of opening their own distribution branches throughout the developing world. By the early 1920s, U.S. companies established their own branches in Latin America, encountering only mild competition from European and local distributors (Schnitman, 1980). In the process, the new medium assumed a more defined narrative function and managed to capture the attention and later the devotion of the middle and upper-middle class sectors. These growing and upwardly mobile social sectors became regular consumers of film as entertainment.

The U.S. domination of screen time in Latin America remained unchanged after the advent of sound. By 1935, 76.6% of the 504 feature films released in Argentina were distributed by American firms. In Mexico, 80% of the films presented for censorship review in 1938 originated in the U.S. This domination is the historical root of one of the most pervasive problems faced by local film industries in Latin America, and it persists today. Insofar as the exhibition sector grew through a steady supply of foreign films, Latin American exhibitors always demanded a free flow of foreign productions.

Exhibition

In Latin America, the development of an exhibition market followed the population growth and was related to the social and cultural characteristics of the various countries. Generally speaking, Argentina, Brazil, and Mexico lead the way in terms of size of their domestic markets; Chile, Colombia, Peru, and Venezuela represent intermediate markets, while the film market in the rest of the Latin American countries is small (Table 1). Although declining since the introduction of television, film exhibition is still fairly important in Latin America, and is organized into theatre "chains"[1] usually under the ownership of local capital, although the large U.S.-based companies own showcase theatres in several Latin American capitals. Operating in a general business context organized around competition and profit,[2] exhibitors are more concerned with the box office appeal of films than with their national origins, unless a film's nationality is also an element of its attractiveness.

From the point of view of the film exhibition market, three audience sectors can be distinguished in Latin America: the upper classes, the urban middle sectors, and the urban and rural working classes and other low income sectors. In many Latin American countries, it is not unusual to find a relatively high rate of functional illiteracy among the latter group of cinema goers. Traditionally, this has been the section of the public partial to local productions since the advent of sound. On the other hand, under normal censorship conditions, the middle classes tend to prefer foreign films. Since the most powerful local exhibitors cater principally to the middle sectors that provide most of their income, they tend to form close alliances with foreign distributors. Consequently, exhibitors have always opposed most forms of state protectionism for local film production.[3]

Distribution

The world predominance of U.S.-based multinationals in the area of film is a well-established fact (Guback, 1969, 1976, 1979). The basic mechanisms of this dominance rely on the multinationals' control of the main distribution channels, established in turn on these companies' access to several financial sources for film production (Chanan, 1980; Gordon, 1976). Branches of the large U.S.-based producers-distributors dominate

[1] "Chain" refers to theatres under common ownership or control, while "release tracks" refer to theaters' release agreements that do not necessarily assume such common ownership or control.

[2] This context does not apply in the case of Cuba, whose film industry has seen a remarkable development in an economy guided by different principles.

[3] In some cases, state protectionist measures have been accompanied by closer government inspection of theatres' box offices and tax payments.

the largest portion of the film markets in all Latin American countries except Cuba. These companies distribute not only American films, but they also, at least since the mid-1950s, have distributed a large number of European productions for which special financial or distribution arrangements were made.

Typically, Latin American countries have a tightly-knit clique of U.S.-based distribution companies, sometimes a few branches of firms based in Europe, and a variable number of local distributors marketing local, European, and some minor U.S. productions. The American group is clearly the most powerful—organized in the United States in the Motion Picture Export Association (MPEA) (Guback, 1969), and locally in each Latin American country of importance as film boards of trade integrated through the local representatives of the U.S. film companies. These organizations are prepared to defend their interests at whatever governmental level is deemed necessary. The MPEA and its local branches basic philosophy is "free trade." In the area of film, free trade can be translated as freedom to introduce in the Latin American countries as many pictures as the local markets will bear, and exchange and remit abroad the revenues accrued in local currencies.

It goes without saying that the MPEA and its local representatives oppose all attempts at state protectionism for local film industries. In most cases they also oppose government-imposed ceilings on the price of theatre tickets, as these ceilings favor the sectors of the public that are not their primary clients. They also oppose measures intended to control the outward flow of foreign currency and, interestingly enough, in some cases protest and oppose censorship practices that tend to curtail the commercial appeal of some of their films, although censorship is usually harsher for local productions.

MPEA's free trade philosophy dovetails perfectly with the free trade orientation of powerful fractions of the Latin American elite. For these elite sectors, usually linked to the production or commercialization of basic exports, free trade means the ability to trade abroad with fewer state impositions, including the importation of foreign goods for local consumption.

Historically, the distribution systems of national and foreign films have differed. Latin American films were distributed for flat fees in the interior and in foreign markets, while U.S.-based distributors could afford to maintain distribution networks that marketed their films for percentages of the gross, coupled with "block-booking" and "blind-booking" (Schnitman, 1981, p. 265). Although there is a recent trend to distribute both local and foreign films through the percentage system, this system is still very difficult to control in various regions of the Latin American interior.

Production

The production of feature films in Latin America has fluctuated according to the various countries' domestic and foreign markets, the general cycle of economic development, and competition with television.

Several countries were active in local production in the era of silent movies which were undertaken by many small firms since the investments required were relatively modest. With the advent of sound, only Argentina, Brazil, and Mexico saw the transition to large studios turning out local features. These countries had a certain industrial base, and their domestic markets for film expanded as a consequence of import-substitution industrialization processes. The fraction of the film market encompassing the popular sectors also expanded as a consequence of the widespread internal migration from rural to urban areas that accompanied industrialization.

The life of the studio system in these countries was short, and was linked to the activation of domestic Latin American markets brought about by World War II, and extended for a few years after the war. Since the diffusion of television in the early 1960s, most local film production has been undertaken by independent producers.

POLITICAL ASPECTS

Given the dominance of foreign distributors in the Latin American film markets, the most important political variables that can *directly* affect the growth of local film industries are: (1) the existence, characteristics, and mode of implementation of state protectionist policies for local productions, and (2) the mode of censorship operation. Protectionism and censorship can be seen as having a direct effect on film production, but the general economic and political climate affects local filmmaking in a variety of direct and indirect ways. In more specific terms, the rate of exchange at which film stock is imported and the enactment of price ceilings for theatre tickets are also political measures that directly affect local filmmaking. Ideally, the above aspects should be part of general and comprehensive communication policies that, as such, have not been developed in the region.

Protectionism

Protectionism can be defined as a government policy designed to encourage or maintain industries which are endangered by foreign competition. Protectionism for Latin American film industries does exist and has existed under different forms and with variable effects. When most effective, it has been associated with the cycles of growth of the fractions of the local bourgeoisies that produce for the domestic market through import substitution. As would be expected, local production groups and film workers' trade unions have always attempted to pressure governments toward protectionist policies.

In the following chapters, the quantitative analysis of Latin American film industries' output will clearly show that state protectionism can favor the growth of local production, and can be considered a necessary but not sufficient condition for the development of local cultural industries (Schnitman, 1980, 1981). The "infant industry argument" might apply here. According to this argument, an industry does not operate optimally until certain economies of scale have been reached (Bannock et al., 1977, p. 215). In a small country, a film industry might not be viable on economic considerations alone, but then cultural considerations can be brought into play, as well as the need to protect at least part of the domestic market.

Various forms and degrees of state protectionism for local film production exist today in Latin America. These protectionist measures tend to vary greatly in their content and implementation, both across countries and within countries whenever governments change. They have been basically consistent and continued in Mexico from 1936 onwards, in Argentina from 1944 to 1955 (Schnitman, 1980), in Brazil since the early 1970s (Johnson, 1982a, b), and are a relatively recent phenomenon in Colombia, Panamá, and Venezuela.

Censorship

Film censorship in Latin America is traditionally justified on moral grounds, for the protection of minors, etc. In practice, however, in most Latin American countries censorship boards take a dim view of oppositional ideologies expressed in film. Censorship in Latin America is one more area of political struggle among social groups wishing to advance different cultural projects. It oscillates between a normal state of tight repression of most forms of social and political criticism and brief interludes of liberalization, depending upon the general orientation of the various governments.

The notion of aesthetic labor is relevant here (Chanan, 1980, pp. 119–21). Insofar as the production of the content of cultural forms cannot be completely mechanized, and wide portions of it rest within the judgment of the makers of cultural products, formal and ideological controls become necessary. Carrying this notion further, it can be postulated that the peculiar mode of production (the way aesthetic labor is articulated) within each medium entails different forms of institutional control. Insofar as the means of production are relatively more decentralized in film than in other mass media, like radio and television, dominant forces find formal censorship necessary in order to ensure a certain level of congruence between mass-mediated messages in film and current social arrangements. Censorship systems vary greatly among Latin American countries, although all perform the task as defined above. Latin American governments can also rely on other resources to influence film content (discrimination in terms of credit sources, state subsidies, etc.). In some cases, exhibitors have refused to show local films because of their critical content (Chapter 6).

Several authors in different Latin American countries have pointed out that censorship organizations tend to judge local productions more harshly than foreign ones. In Argentina, for instance, before the November 1983 election that brought Alfonsín to the presidency, there was a clear double standard in censorship that made audiences shy away from local productions (Tabbia, 1979). Although the double standard of censorship is a variable located at the politico-cultural level of analysis, it tends to discourage certain forms of local production, thus having an economic effect on national film industries.

CULTURAL ASPECTS

The fractions of the domestic exhibition markets distinguished above need to be recalled here (upper classes, middle sectors, and rural and urban working classes). The more cosmopolitan outlook of upper and middle sectors have conditioned them to expect technical, narrative, and formal standards that characterize the products of the film industries of the advanced capitalist countries. Previous experience, based on a long history of advanced cinematographies' worldwide screen time domination and local censorship double standards, has caused Latin American middle sectors to frame their expectations of feature films in terms that foreign distributors are better equipped to satisfy.

The sectors of the public where urban and rural workers and other low income sectors predominate, however, have been more resistant to foreign cultural forms. In many Latin American countries, social class distinctions overlap to a large extent with ethnic differences, making cultural distinctions across social classes more marked. Insofar as identification is one of the basic mechanisms of consumption of the dominant film form, foreign dubbed films have encountered widespread resistance among spectators belonging to the less affluent socioeconomic groups due to wide linguistic and cultural differences and the ensuing identification difficulties. In the early 1930s, Hollywood companies attempted, without success, to reach this sector of the Latin American market with Spanish-speaking films made in the U.S.[4] (Chapter 4).

In Latin America, the feature film as a mass medium contributed to the relative internationalization of the middle sectors' cultural taste. As a hypothesis, it can be postulated that television reinforced this process, and initiated the relative internationalization of mass-mediated cultural taste for urban and rural popular sectors.[5] This relative internationalization defines a "frame" (Goffman, 1974) or set of expectations concerning not only film content but also the generally dominant use of the medium as cultural form. In other words, it defines what a film should be and the elements it should contain in order to qualify as an acceptable cultural commodity. The above refers to technical and formal standards, and to the definition of feature films as conveyors of "fiction" in its various "genre" conventions, as opposed to the possibilities of documentaries and other forms of film essay, whose mode of representation has been relegated to newsreels and shorts by the institutional organization of the predominantly commercial use of the medium.[6]

Both film and television have potentialities for much wider uses, but their frames of utilization are defined in the cultural productive practices of the advanced capitalist countries, and then exported. Once exported, however, it is the complex, receiving social formations that set the limits to the use of the new communication media, and these limits can either contract or expand, as the following chapters show.

In Latin America, the potential for local film production and distribution has always had to compete with the standards set by foreign productions, standards originated in social formations that historically benefited from sustained processes of accumulation of capital, human resources, and technical expertise. The domination of Latin American domestic film markets by foreign products and distributors has been and continues to be a basic element affecting not only local production perspectives of quantitative growth, but also local producers' choice of content and the overall organization of film as cultural form.

---

[4] There is a remarkable diversity in the forms of spoken Spanish in the various Latin American countries. Only the relatively recent wide diffussion of television prompted the standardization of a form purified of localisms, called "neutral Spanish," utilized in television dubbed programs.

[5] For a discussion of hybrid cultural forms in developing countries' mass media see Tunstall, 1977, pp. 273-75.

[6] In the same way that fiction is not the only way of writing, although it may be the dominant cultural form in the area of social practice called "literature" in modern society, fiction feature films are not the only possible way of using the medium.

STRATEGIES FOR SURVIVAL

Facing domestic markets dominated by the large U.S.-based multinational corporations, Latin American producers and filmmakers have followed four basic strategies:

1. Make films for the fraction of the market not reached by foreign films, concentrating on aspects of local society and folklore, and on forms of comedy heavily dependent on wordplay. The limit to this strategy is determined by the popular audiences' limited incomes, unless there is also a foreign market, as is the case for Mexico, an exporter not only to other Latin American countries, but also to the growing Latino market in the U.S.
2. Attempt to compete with foreign productions for the more profitable middle- and upper-class public, depicting similar content (internationalization of both form and content). This solution is typically undertaken either as a risky venture, or under very supportive protectionism.
3. Make films aimed at the local middle-classes, centered on "localized" middle-class concerns (localization of content and internationalization of form).
4. Make films outside normal commercial channels.

Historically, all of the above strategies have been followed both alternately and simultaneously in Latin America.[7] Concerning the first strategy, for instance, in the era of silent films the visual "localization" (attempt to make local) of Latin American films was often centered on the dress and customs of *gauchos* in Argentina, *huasos* in Chile, *charros* in Mexico, and the Indian population in Brazil and Bolivia. With the advent of sound, this strategy meant the inclusion of local forms of speech in local films, and songs based on folk cultural forms as reprocessed, mass-mediated, and diffused by radio.

While the above line of production has continued more or less uninterruptedly in Argentina, Brazil, and Mexico, beginning in the years of World War II local producers attempted to reach middle-class audiences with films based on the classics of world literature. These attempts were possible because of state protectionism or because markets were protected by the war situation. As a rule, these productions failed to attract the Latin

[7] This does not imply that Latin American critical and/or "underground" films are principally a different commercial strategy; these films usually spring from different cultural-ideological commitments than commercial ones.

American middle classes, and were not always in favor among the popular sectors of cinema goers. It should be noted, however, that even then many films combining local milieus and a social-critical perspective were successful and attracted various sectors of the public. But this orientation only surfaces sporadically, and is strongly discouraged through censorship and other methods of government control.

The underground production of critical feature films is a relatively recent phenomenon, dating from the mid-1960s, although critical shorts and documentaries have a long history in Latin America (see Burton, 1978). The production of such films is only possible under certain conditions and constitutes a marginal solution vis-a-vis commercial exhibition circuits. (These films are shown mostly in film clubs, trade unions, universities, and political party facilities.)

This introductory presentation does not aim to give the impression of a monolithic and oppressive situation, completely devoid of alternatives. Films are being made in Latin America, and not always of the innocuous variety. The following chapters trace the differing courses that national film production followed in Argentina, Brazil, and Mexico, the Latin American countries with relatively large domestic markets, taking into account their respective historical frameworks. In subsequent chapters, the cases of Chile and Bolivia illustrate the alternatives of national film policies and national film production in countries that have intermediate and small markets.

Chapter 2
The Silent Years, 1896–1930

The dependency approach in social sciences can be interpreted as a conceptualization of the consequences for peripheral societies of the changes in capitalism as a world system from about the 1870s. For peripheral and semiperipheral countries, capitalist dependent development would be the consequence of the expansion of capitalism presented in the classical theory of imperialism (Cardoso, 1977).[1] The characteristics of this new stage in the development of capitalism as a world system were directly relevant to the way the innovation of film developed, was institutionally organized, and was exported on a worldwide basis. Film was born with an international vocation, as demanded by its times. The innovation had a rapid diffusion as a novelty, but the technical capability of providing all the necessary means of production remained concentrated in the advanced capitalist countries.

Choosing to frame the present study within a dependency perspective entails paying special attention to the international and domestic contexts for film-related activities in Latin America. The following section is a brief introduction to the international framework within which Latin American film industries were forced to develop in the era of silent cinema,

[1] An unsympathetic but informative view of the various trends in the dependency approach can be found in Packenham (1978). Fejes (1981) reviewed various dependency approaches from the perspective of communication studies. Basic features of the dependency approach are discussed in Cardoso and Faletto (1979) (see especially their new Introduction to the English edition) and Chilcote and Edelstein (1974).

while Chapter 3 focuses on the international context relevant to the era of the "talkies." (For a more detailed view, see Sadoul, 1973; Balio, 1976; Conant, 1960; and Guback, 1979.)

THE STRUGGLE FOR MARKETS, 1896–1930

In the U.S., Edison equipment was used for the first screening of a film in a New York music hall in April 1896. A few months earlier, in France, the Lumière brothers had organized the first film show in Paris during the Christmas season of 1895. The success of such a novelty produced the rapid expansion of the Lumière organization in Europe and its attempt to enter the United States market. The Lumière films were shown in New York in June, 1896, but six months later, when a Lumière representative tried to repeat the show, the city was well supplied with facilities equipped with U.S.-patented projectors, and the Lumière show was cancelled under the threat of judicial prosecution (Jobes, 1966, p. 29). This event foreshadowed the atmosphere of competition for national and international markets that would soon follow.

The French film industry enjoyed an accelerated development until World War I. Its domestic market during that period, was dominated by the Pathé, Gaumont, and Méliès organizations. Pathé took on the characteristics of a large organization with an international distribution network (Pathé and Lumière not only manufactured films, but also cameras and projectors, as was the case with Edison, and others in the United States.)

Before World War I, many countries witnessed the beginnings of indigenous film industries, for example, Denmark, Italy, and Sweden. World War I, however, helped the development of the U.S. film industry, which took over a growing portion of the European market, while the film industries in Europe were paralyzed by the international conflict. At the end of the war, U.S. distributors were dominant in the most important European domestic markets. Moreover, British, French, and other producers found it difficult to regain a foothold on their home grounds, and found their former U.S. markets, where vast consolidations were taking place, practically closed to their films.

Two stages in the development of the U.S. film industry can be distinguished. From 1896 to 1908, when film was a medium requiring relatively small investments, there was a good deal of competition for the different aspects of the new industry. The period from 1908 to 1930 can be seen as the development of the industry into a virtual oligopolic structure. It was at the beginning of this period that Edison attempted to organize the U.S. film market on the basis of patent rights.

Edison's goal was to control as many aspects as possible of the film business in the United States, and his organization almost succeeded in 1908, when the Motion Pictures Patent Company (MPPC) was formed. Under Edison's control, this combination integrated all the U.S. and foreign companies that agreed to pay patent rights to Edison. Pathé and Méliès, from France, were part of the MPPC.

However, the "Trust" (as the Motion Pictures Patent Company was called by the independent producers, distributors, and exhibitors who refused to pay royalties) could not, in practice, prevent independent producers from working, or prevent independent distributors and exhibitors from going into production. Working in Hollywood, these independents gave birth to some of the large companies that have dominated the U.S. and international markets ever since.

In 1912, the U.S. government filed an antitrust action against MPPC to enjoin continuance of the combine. The resulting judicial decision against the combine's monopolistic practices in the commerce of films, cameras, projectors, and accessories gave new momentum to the development of the independents. By 1915, the MPPC was losing control of the industry and it was formally dissolved in 1918 (Conant, 1960, p. 20).

On the strength of two innovations, the star system and the feature film, the independents were in a good position to attempt their own control of the U.S. domestic market. The independents' approach to the control of the United States' domestic market wasn't based, as in the case of Edison, on ownership of patent rights, but on the integration of as many phases in the process of film production and marketing as possible. In horizontal integration processes, weaker companies at any level (production-distribution-exhibition) were purchased by stronger companies at the same level. Vertical integration processes took place when producers secured distribution and exhibition facilities for themselves, and exhibitors went into production and distribution.[2]

The investments necessary for the transition to sound movies and the 1929 economic crisis furthered the centralization process already underway; from that moment on, five companies dominated the industry, forming an original oligopolic structure: Paramount, Metro-Goldwyn-Mayer (MGM), 20th Century Fox, Warner Bros., and Radio-Keith-Orpheum (RKO). In contrast, Columbia, Universal, and United Artists were considered relatively minor powers as they did not own important theatre chains in the United States, although they were significant exporters to

[2] "Moving from opposite ends of the business, producers continued to buy up film exchanges and cinemas to ensure an outlet for their products, and theatre owners acquired production companies to guarantee a regular supply of films at reasonable rentals" (French, 1971, p. 25). For a general view of the processes of capitalist accumulation, concentration, centralization, and horizontal and vertical integration, not limited to the film industry, see Sweezy, 1956, Ch. 14.

other countries. Control of the most important sectors of the domestic market in the United States gave these companies the necessary base for the dominance of the main sectors of the domestic markets of other countries, both advanced and developing.

To summarize, in the period from 1908 to 1930, the U.S. film industry evolved into a "mature oligopoly" (Balio, 1976, p. 313). By the 1920s the large U.S. companies emerged as the most powerful in the world. Utilizing their own distribution channels, these companies controlled the most important portion of the domestic market in the U.S. and significant parts of the domestic markets of other countries, thus reducing the potential market where other national producers could recover their investments.

FILM IN LATIN AMERICA:
THE SILENT YEARS

When, by the end of December 1895, the Lumière brothers had launched their first public show of the *Cinématographe* in Paris, they had a much wider public in mind. Operating within a capitalist context that increasingly required a world-view approach to the launching of innovations, the Lumières did not present their *Cinématographe* in public until they had enough equipment and trained operators to undertake a worldwide campaign (Sadoul, 1964, pp. 55–76). Barnouw and Krishnaswamy (1980, p. 3) stated that "... Lumière *opérateurs,* with instructions to withhold the secrets of their equipment from everyone including kings and beautiful women, began crisscrossing the globe—Europe, America, Africa, Asia, Australia. Other traveling showmen were close behind, sometimes ahead, as the *cinématographe* expeditions sped to major world centers." Several inventors had been working along similar lines, toward the goal of a viable film camera-projector, and soon other systems appeared in the world market.

The most cosmopolitan Latin American capitals were in relatively close contact with the various world metropoles, and the innovation was shown in Buenos Aires, Mexico City, and Rio de Janeiro only a few months after being demonstrated in Paris. In Argentina, for instance, Lumière and other films were shown for the first time in September 1896 (Di Nubila, 1959, Vol. I, p. 15). One year later, French Gaumont cameras, projectors, and films were imported. Cameras, films, film stock, and projectors were imported from France, and later from the United States. By 1908, many local distributors were handling foreign films, and most of them also produced and distributed short Argentine features, documentaries, and advertisement films. World War I had a stimulating effect on Argentine film activity. Local production soared between 1916 and 1919, declining after that until the decade of the 1930s, and it can be safely assumed that during the 1916–1919 period local film production benefited from the interruption in the flow of European films.[3]

In Brazil, the first film show took place in 1896, with equipment called Omnió(grafo (Gonzaga and Salles Gomes, 1966, p. 15). The first theatre was opened in Rio de Janeiro in 1897, but until 1906 growth was very slow due to the unreliable supply of electric power. In 1907, new power sources had an immediate effect on film exhibition, and several theatres were opened in Rio in the second half of that year. Some of the new exhibitors (most of them European immigrants) attempted to deal simultaneously in film exhibition, distribution of imports, and production, creating a local form of vertical integration and an upsurge of vitality in filmmaking between 1908 and 1911. This trend was shortlived, and further specialization of functions undermined local filmmaking.

World War I resulted in some restimulating local film production, including an active movement of regional filmmaking. Starting from a very low point in 1912–1914, Brazilian production peaked in 1917 with 16 films made, but fell abruptly in 1918 (Gonzaga and Salles Gomes, 1966, p. 36). Local production found it difficult to find exhibitors, and the press treated Brazilian filmmaking as a marginal activity.

Although there were qualitative improvements, and a renewed momentum for local production in São Paulo, Brazilian film production would have to wait until the arrival of sound to regain a fraction of its domestic market. It is also a good illustration of the innovation-gap phenomenon to note that in Brazil, as in other Latin American countries, by the end of the 1920s local filmmakers had attained a good mastery of the narrative language in silent films, but "this mastery was attained by 1928, when all the cinematographic language laboriously built during twenty years in Europe and the U.S. was condemned by the sonorized film revolution" (Gonzaga and Salles Gomes, 1966, p. 61).

In Mexico, the engineer Salvador Toscano bought equipment from the Lumière representative in Mexico in 1897, exhibited the same films shown by Lumière in Paris, and soon started making his own films. Local production grew very slowly, but here also the effects of World War I boosted local filmmaking, and film production increased after 1915, reaching what may be considered the golden age of Mexico's silent cinema between 1918 and 1923 (*Diccionario Porrua,* 1964, pp. 310–11).

In the silent film era, the development of local film production in an intermediate country like Chile did not differ very much from the pattern

---

[3] The best opportunities for industrial development in capitalist-dependent countries occurred when the traditional pattern of relations with the dominant capitalist countries was interrupted or weakened. When world wars or international economic crises weakened the Latin American countries' ability to import, the scarcity of imported products created a gap that local producers attempted to fill.

followed in the larger countries (Table 2). Bolivia, on the other hand, with its relatively small domestic market, shows clear differences. Eighty local feature films were released in Chile from 1916 to 1931, and production peaked in the 1924-1926 years (Godoy Quezada, 1966), although it should be remembered that "in these years the production of a film did not involve a large amount of capital, and it was more an artisan than an industrial enterprise" (Ossa Coo, 1971, p. 22). Films were made, however, that won national success and international recognition. The potential for the improvement of local production was there, but had to compete with the standards of foreign production, and technical conditions in Chile were extremely precarious. In 1924, for instance, the mechanically gifted cameraman of a successful Chilean film had to build his own camera piece by piece (Ossa Coo, 1971, p. 24).

In Bolivia, the first film show took place in 1909, brought by two Italian entrepreneurs living in Peru, not in La Paz but in Guaqui, a small port on Titicaca lake (Mesa G., 1976, 1979). *Corazón Aymará* (Aymara Heart), released in 1925, is usually considered the first Bolivian feature. It was based on a novel that attempted to reflect the problems of a section of the Indian population. A total of four Bolivian feature films were released from 1925 to 1931, of which three centered on contemporary or historical aspects of the Indian population, a distinctive concern that would be reassumed later on by filmmakers of other generations and ideological outlooks.

DISTRIBUTION OF U.S. FILMS IN LATIN AMERICA

During approximately the first 25 years of the silent film era (1896-1920), foreign films in Latin America were distributed by local firms. U.S. and other foreign companies, however, aspired to establish their own branches and wanted to deal directly with local exhibitors to avoid sharing profits with local distributors. In the early 1920s, most of the large U.S.-based film companies began to establish distribution branches in the various Latin American countries, where they encountered relatively mild competition from some European representatives and local distributors (Schnitman, 1979, p. 49; Turner, 1968, p. 298; Usabel, 1975, Chs. 2 and 3).

Latin American distributors, who until then had been handling both U.S. and European features, were understandable unhappy with the new developments that short-circuited their traditional relationship with exhibitors. Glucksman, a local distributor from Argentina, who relayed U.S., European, and some local films to Chile, Uruguay, Paraguay, Peru, Bolivia, and Ecuador, and who maintained a permanent office in New York and some European cities, wrote:

The demand for American movies continues strong . . . The outlook is so good that the larger companies are considering more seriously than ever the establishment of additional distributing organizations of their own in the foreign markets, even in the smaller territories. This generally means that an American manager is sent to take charge of the business . . . As the American concerns take hold in the foreign markets, the business of the local distributors is decreased and in some cases entirely destroyed . . . The exhibitors in different territories are beginning to resent the foreign invasion that seems to take the aspect of an American monopoly of the local motion picture business . . . The local distributors, in order to exist, are obliged to increase their purchase of European-made material. This material is gradually obtaining greater acceptance because the exhibitors prefer to do business with their old established friends rather than with foreigners (*Film Daily Yearbook,* 1925, p. 661).

A very different point of view was expressed the same year by a representative of Fox who stated:

It is being realized to a greater extent every day that American producers and distributors are not trespassers in foreign territory, but on the contrary, have every desire to cooperate and assist the foreign exhibitor to increase his revenue at the box-office . . . (*Film Daily Yearbook,* 1925, p. 661).

Gluckman's predictions proved to be incorrect, and a 1928 report informed its readers that "American films average nearly 90 percent of all shows throughout Latin America and there is little evidence to indicate that this supremacy will be threatened in the near future" (*Film Daily Yearbook,* 1928, pp. 942–43).

The superior economic and political leverage of the U.S.-based companies, the attractiveness of their products, and their advanced advertising techniques were factors difficult to overcome. As a sign of the U.S. film companies ability to utilize the mechanisms of the U.S. government, besides their own resources, it is relevant to note that the 1925–1926 U.S. Congress appropriated a special fund for the creation of a Motion Picture Section in the Bureau of Foreign and Domestic Commerce: "In general the Motion Picture Section endeavors to serve the industry in every legitimate way in maintaining and developing the exhibition of American motion pictures in foreign markets" (*Film Daily Yearbook,* 1927, p. 925).

By the end of the 1920s, when all film-related activities had to face the transition toward the technology of sound, the large U.S. companies were well entrenched in the most important Latin American markets. In Argentina, for instance, the first available distribution data, covering the second half of 1931, show that, with the sole exception of RKO, all the important U.S. companies were already active in the Argentine market, competing with the European firms Terra (Germany), Filmreich (Germany), Gaumont British (England), and local distributors (Table 4). By 1931, all the large U.S. companies had established direct branches not only in Buenos Aires but also in the most important cities of the Argentine interior: Bahia Blanca, Rosario, Santa Fe, and Cordoba. The principles on which the U.S. distributors operated in Argentina were the same that were in use in the United States domestic market from around 1916: distribution to exhibitors on a rental basis, blind-booking, and block-booking. Blind-booking meant that, in most cases, exhibitors had to book films without the benefit of a previous screening. This practice was coupled to block-booking, by which exhibitors had to book films in blocks containing a few near-certain box office successes, while most of the block consisted of pictures that, if offered individually, would find fewer takers.

Argentine film producers, on the other hand, could not go beyond a primitive distribution system that involved selling a film to regional distributors, who acquired the right to lease the picture to theatres in a determined geographical area. Such a procedure reduced local producer's chances of sharing in any unusual profits that might appear on the distribution-exhibition level. The large foreign distributors had their own distribution network in the provinces, and a much better bargaining position vis-a-vis exhibitors, based on the quantity and attractiveness of the films they could offer, and they were in a better position to demand a percentage of the gross.

PROSPECTS FOR FILM PRODUCTION IN LATIN AMERICA 1896–1930: A SUMMARY

To summarize, one of the most important aspects of Latin American film production in the international context was the development of film as a mass entertainment industry in the U.S. and Europe. Film activities in the various Latin American countries evolved in a context of capitalist-dependent development where the capitalist aspect created an environment of competition and the struggle for profits, and dependency meant (among other things) that all the necessary means of production had to be imported and that local production had to face domestic markets dominated by the products of the advanced capitalist countries.

Local entrepreneurs had to approach filmmaking as an import-substitution process, and such processes were favored when the government implemented deliberate protectionist programs or when the World Wars or economic depressions disrupted the exchange patterns between advanced and dependent capitalist countries. Speaking in broad terms, however, from 1896 to 1930 all film-related activities in Latin America took place under governments espousing the view that the role of Latin American countries in the world economy was as producers of primary products and importers of industrial goods. This view was embodied in the ideas of free trade and non-intervention of the state in the economy, and did not favor state protectionism.

During World War I, the interruption in the flow of European films created the first opportunity for local producers to fill the gap. No protectionist structure existed at the time, however, and local film production declined after the war in most Latin American countries, due to the resumption of the dominant presence of foreign films in their domestic markets. Most of the entrepreneurs who entered the film world did so as an extension of retail businesses concerned with photographic equipment, as exhibitors, or as technicians who could operate cameras and projectors. Most were recent European immigrants[4] determined to make their fortunes in Latin America, and prepared to try innovative industrial and commercial activities that were looked down upon by the ruling "criollo" landholding elites. Active and open to innovation, they lacked, however, the political power or influence to demand state protection.

Several of the entrepreneurs started out simultaneously as producers, distributors, and exhibitors, but later (especially after World War I) specialized as distributors and/or exhibitors, the most stable part of the business considering that film production and distribution remained in the hands of large foreign companies, reflecting an international division of labor that concentrated technical innovation, research, and most industrial production in advanced capitalist countries. In other words, local film entrepreneurs found it more profitable to specialize as commercial bourgeoisie than as industrial bourgeoisie, even though the commercial success of some Latin American films of the silent era indicated that the potential was there. It is clear, then, that film as an innovation found a completely different fate in the two Americas. While the U.S. had the technical, financial, and market size conditions to allow for innovation in its production, distribution, and exhibition aspects, Latin American dependent capitalism could only develop its distribution and exhibition aspects on the basis of foreign films, to the detriment of local production.

Under the above conditions, and in order to attempt to gain some competitive edge, in many cases Latin American film producers and directors followed one or more of these strategies:

[4] In many cases, Italian immigrants displaced by World War I were the initiators of narrative filmmaking in Latin America. This might be related to the remarkable development of film production in Italy prior to that war.

1. Emphasis on local scenes, history, speech, and music (in the silent era through records and live music);
2. Depiction of contemporary sensational murders, and other crimes with sexual or scandalous overtones; and,
3. Incorporation of elements of political satire or social denunciation.

Insofar as censorship made the last two courses of action a risky venture, an often superficial emphasis on the local interests remained a major strategy of Latin American filmmakers, both during the silent era and in the early era of the "talkies."

Chapter 3
The International Context

This chapter offers a brief overview of the main forces in the international production and marketing of films, as a preliminary context for focusing on the film industries of selected Latin American countries in the following chapters. As noted previously, the U.S. film industry was the most important agent in Latin American distribution markets. Although culturally important, European productions have only intermittently captured a smaller portion of the market in some Latin American countries, while in others the dominance of the U.S. film industry has been almost total. The decades of the 1930s and 1940s saw the continuation of the trend which, aided by the devastating effects of both World Wars on the European cinematographies, gave the American film industry complete control of its own domestic market, and of substantial portions of the domestic markets of other countries, both advanced and developing. The international dominance of the U.S. film industry was a basic element of the framework within which the Latin American film industries attempted their development after the advent of sound.

THE U.S. FILM INDUSTRY, 1930–1948: THE ADVENT OF SOUND

Sound in movies was a factor that strongly reinforced the trend toward economic concentration in the American film industry because it necessitated large investments in the reequipment of studios and theatres. These large investments brought to Hollywood both the companies holding patent rights for the sound systems and the powerful banks capable of advancing the funds required by the new equipment.[1]

By the early 1930s the trend toward horizontal and vertical integration had crystallized into a well-organized oligopoly, and the U.S. screen was dominated by five companies: Warner Bros., Metro-Goldwyn-Mayer, Paramount, Radio-Keith-Orpheum (RKO), and 20th Century Fox. Each of these companies produced from 40 to 60 films per year, and together they owned or controlled the principal theatres in urban areas, theatres that yielded nearly 70% of the box office receipts in the U.S. (Balio, 1976, p. 213). Universal, Columbia, and United Artists were considered relatively minor powers, the first two being production and distribution concerns that did not control significant exhibition facilities, and the latter being only a distribution organization for independent producers. These three companies were minor only relative to the "big five." In developing countries they released significant numbers of films (see, for example, Table 5).

Although the use of sound in movies hastened the process of economic concentration in the U.S. film industry, it gave new possibilities to the development of local film production in Europe, Latin America, and elsewhere. German producer-distributors, for instance, relying on their own sound systems and patents, started making inroads into markets outside their national borders. Some characteristics of the U.S. film industry, however, determined its continued international dominance from the 1930s on.

The United States has had the largest domestic film market in the capitalist world, a market where investments in film could be amortized before sending the film abroad. Local amortization meant that, when entering foreign markets, the American productions had to recover only distribution costs incurred in the new market, while local film entrepreneurs had to recover both production and distribution costs in the same market. While foreign markets were highly vulnerable, the U.S. domestic market was practically impenetrable to foreign producers and distributors who tried unsuccessfully to establish their own distribution outlets in the United States (Guback, 1969, p. 83).

The relative inaccessibility of the U.S. domestic market, that could be reached only partially through American distributors, was not the result of deliberate government protectionism but a result of the vertical integra-

[1] The patent rights for the new sound systems were held by Western Electric, a subsidiary of American Telephone and Telegraph (AT&T), and Radio Corporation of America (RCA), with links to the Rockefeller financial group (Huettig, 1944, p. 4).

tion of the American film industry that reserved the most important chains of theatres for the products of the producer-distributors who owned or controlled these theatres as outlets for their films. Control of their domestic market provided large U.S. companies with a basis for the penetration of the domestic markets of other countries, both advanced (like the European countries) and developing. Whenever possible and profitable, distribution of American films in foreign countries was handled through direct branches of the large U.S. companies.

In addition, the U.S. was the first country to standardize film production, and its film industry had the financial capability, not only to satisfy a demand, but also to at least partially create that demand through the most powerful advertising apparatus in the world.

Another important factor in the international predominance of the American film companies was the regulation of competition among the companies through the offices of the Motion Picture Producers and Distributors of America (MPPDA), whose foreign department was in charge of arranging for the continuous and unhindered operation of U.S. companies abroad and regulating their competition in foreign markets. The MPPDA was organized in 1921, principally to present a better image of the film industry to its public and the government, and to prevent the possibility of a censorship organization being created outside the industry's control. MPPDA was largely successful in representing the interests of the U.S. film industry in negotiations with various institutions, both government and private. It also acted as mediator in cases of intra-industry conflict.

MPPDA's Foreign Department was in charge of trying to keep foreign distribution channels open for U.S. films, and of informing Hollywood about the activities of foreign censors. By the mid-1930s, the MPPDA maintained a Washington, D.C. office, where the head of its foreign department spent about half of his time, due to the fact that "in dealing with other governments on matters pertaining to quotas, tariffs, and exchange restrictions [the Foreign Department] works mostly through the Department of State" (*Fortune*, Dec. 1938). The name of the organization was changed to Motion Picture Association of America (MPAA) in 1945. At that time the companies represented in the MPAA felt the need for an organization dealing exclusively with the problems of the industry abroad, so the Motion Picture Export Association (MPEA) was created. MPEA's objectives were to operate as a legal cartel representing the U.S. film industry interests abroad, demanding free competition, open access to markets, and unhindered trade (Guback, 1969, p. 5). The MPEA was organized as a legal cartel, following the provisions of the Webb-Pomerene Export Trade Act of 1918. This legislation allows American companies to cooperate in foreign trade following organizational and operational procedures that could otherwise be considered illegal by the antitrust laws aimed at the United States domestic market.

Eric Johnston was appointed MPEA's first president. In his first annual report, Johnston "pointed out that revenue from foreign distribution is the life blood of the American film industry [and] stressed the need for strong Government backing to obtain a free flow of film into foreign countries and surmount numerous industry trade obstacles" (*Variety*, March 27, 1946, p. 21). MPEA's lobbying efforts became a normal aspect of film business activity in Latin America.

THE UNITED STATES FILM INDUSTRY AFTER THE SECOND WORLD WAR

From the late 1940s until the 1970s, the American film industry changed drastically, adjusting to circumstances in its domestic and foreign markets that increased the importance of the latter. The most important of these in the U.S. domestic market were (a.) the wide diffusion of television as the principal form of leisure time entertainment, and (b.) legal actions against the large film companies affecting the companies' vertical integration. Internationally, temporarily frozen dollars in Europe and advantages in costs and subsidies led to an important growth of American-financed film production there. Large U.S. companies continued to dominate the international film markets, primarily through their distribution organizations. These companies became part of important economic conglomerates, or expanded and diversified themselves into conglomerates.

The U.S. Domestic Market

Theatre attendance in the United States underwent a marked reduction after World War II, increasing the importance of foreign markets for the American film industry. The spread of television and its popularity took a heavy toll on theatre attendance, prompting the large film companies to initiate drastic reorganization processes that cut production and budgets. Moreover, these companies had to adjust to the results of legal battles against vertical integration initiated many years earlier by independent producers and exhibitors.

American independent producers, organized in 1932 in the Independent Motion Picture Producers Association (IMPPA), had battled vertical integration, which kept independent productions off of the screens of the circuits of integrated theatres. In 1938, independent producers finally obtained the initiation of legal procedures against the movie majors from the U.S. Department of Justice. Legal procedures progressed slowly, but their net effect was that between 1949 and 1953 the large film companies were forced to separate their production and exhibition activities. A 1948 Supreme Court verdict declared discriminatory pricing and purchasing arrangements favoring affiliated theatres an illegal restraint of trade.

These judicial procedures succeeded in breaking the large companies' vertical integration, but did not significantly reduce their importance in the film business. Meanwhile, Hollywood went from a strategy of competing with television to one of collaboration with the new medium, producing films and serials for TV and selling the rights for the airing of old pictures. Internationally, the financial capability of undertaking vast advertising campaigns and to advance production loans made distribution the key film industry factor, a factor that remained under the hegemony of the large American film companies (Gordon, 1976).

Hollywood Foreign Markets
After World War II

During World War II, Hollywood accumulated an important backlog of pictures and was ready to release them in Europe, its most important foreign market. In order to curb the outflow of dollars deemed necessary to reconstruct their postwar economies, several European countries reimposed protectionist measures, such as screen and distributors' quotas. In addition, the earnings of the American film companies were frozen, leading to the signing of a number of film treaties between the Motion Picture Export Association (MPEA) and certain European governments. Most of these treaties permitted U.S. company branches in Europe to remit about one-third of their annual revenues, while the remainder could be used for investment in film or other business concerns. The U.S. State Department was instrumental in helping the MPEA negotiate these agreements. Frozen funds, lower costs, and European government film production subsidies encouraged the production of American-financed films in Europe.

In order to profit from the European subsidies, the large U.S. companies found ways to comply with the legal requirements imposed by European governments to qualify as "local" producers (Phillips, 1975; Guback, 1976). During the 1950s and 1960s American distributors brought more European films into the United States and other markets, but these films were to a large extent their own products. The trend toward American film production in Europe declined after 1969, due to rising costs there, but U.S. distributors continue to handle the international release of many films made in Europe by European directors.

Film Companies and Conglomerates

Following general economic trends in the United States, many of the large film companies became part of economic conglomerates during the 1960s. To note some instances: in 1966 Paramount became part of Gulf and Western's leisure time group, owner of 400 theatre screens in Canada and over 60 in France. Gulf and Western is itself a vast conglomerate with interests in steel, hydraulics, mining, and plastics. In 1967, United Artists was acquired by Transamerica Corporation, a conglomerate with interests including insurance, car rentals, and data processing. Transamerica sold United Artists to Metro-Goldwyn-Mayer (MGM) in 1981. MGM is not part of a conglomerate, but has transformed itself into one, with interests in hotels and other leisure time industries. Columbia Pictures diversified into record production and distribution and the manufacture of non-gambling pinball machines. (Guback, 1979; Phillips, 1975) In 1982 Columbia Pictures was acquired by the Coca Cola Co.

Becoming part of economic conglomerates has had a positive influence on the economic stability of the large film companies and has furthered favorable treatment of American films in foreign countries (Balio, 1976, p. 31). The films distributed by the large American companies have also found new marketing channels in television, cable and other forms of pay television, home video (both as tapes and discs), commercial airlines flights, etc.

The preceding paragraphs provide a brief overview of the evolution of the large film companies in the United States as crucial actors in the international context in which Latin American film industries developed after 1930. Although the U.S. film industry underwent remarkable transformations during the 1930–1980 period, for all practical purposes the problem of its overwhelming presence in Latin America remained throughout that period, and only decreased somewhat whenever Latin American governments implemented consistent protectionist policies or when specific markets lost their economic appeal due to unfavorable exchange rates and similar problems. The decade of the 1970s has seen a rationalization of U.S. film distribution in Latin America, leading to elimination of branches and consolidation of outlets both within and between companies in order to reduce distribution costs. Branches of the U.S. distribution companies continue distributing, not only the most successful American films, but also important films made in Europe. As a rule, these companies do not accept Latin American films for distribution in other Latin American countries or in the rest of the world.

Chapter 4
Talking Films and New Opportunities: Argentina and Mexico

The advent of sound gave new momentum to film production in some Latin American countries, but the higher levels of capital and technology required introduced a sharper differentiation among countries according to the sizes of their domestic markets, income levels, and other domestic and international economic, political, and cultural factors. While in Argentina, Brazil, and Mexico, local film production managed, amidst great difficulties and always in competition with foreign films, to attain most of the characteristics of an industrial activity, the rest of Latin America found it practically impossible to reach and sustain an industrial level of film production.

Since films produced in Argentina and Mexico were the most important competitors for the fractions of the Latin American markets less penetrated by U.S. or European films, the following sections are an analysis of developments in both countries.

THE TECHNOLOGY OF SOUND

The advent of sound provided a new opportunity for Latin American producers, allowing them to emphasize more distinctive local traits in their films. Before this new potential could be realized, however, it was necessary to master the new technology, to overcome the technological gap that characterizes the relations between advanced and peripheral countries. Serious attempts at developing a local sound technology were made in

Argentina, Colombia, and Mexico, but were soon replaced by more advanced imported equipment. From all over Latin America, film directors and technicians went to Hollywood to gain first-hand experience with this innovation.

We have seen in Chapter 2 that during World War I the interruption in the flow of European films created the first opportunity for local film producers to fill the gap. No protectionist structure existed at the time, however, and local film production declined after the war due to the resumption of the dominant presence of foreign films. The advent of sound gave Argentine and Mexican producers a new opportunity to seize part of their growing domestic markets. What were the social and cultural bases of the demand for national films? In both countries the more affluent sectors of society preferred the products of the advanced capitalist countries' cultural industries, part of a generalized preference for foreign manufactured products. Local film producers, however, could offer a distinctively local product that appealed to specific sectors of the audience, both domestically and in other Latin American countries; rural and urban low-income sectors provided the initial and most sustained momentum for the demand for local films (Garcia Riera, 1969, vol. 2, p. 7; DiNubila, 1959, vol. 1, p. 61).

But even these popular and low-income sectors of the Latin American audiences, that often, due to total or functional illiteracy, could not read subtitles quickly enough, were a target for the large U.S. companies, afraid of losing their non-English speaking audiences with the advent of sound.[1] These companies began producing films in Spanish, and no less than 113 such films were made between 1930 and 1936. These films were Spanish-language versions produced simultaneously with the U.S. originals, or remakes of silent films (both called "foreign versions"), and sometimes, especially in the case of Fox, films made only in Spanish (Pinto, 1973). It was clear, however, that Spanish-speaking films distributed by the large U.S. companies were not intended to replace the subtitled films enjoyed by spectators belonging to the middle and upper social sectors. Eventually, both foreign versions and American dubbed films were discontinued in most of Latin America, as these procedures were not favored by the intended audiences and proved unprofitable. In terms of the cost/success ratio, U.S. producer-distributors found subtitling a most convenient procedure in releasing their films in Latin America, a solution that left out wide sectors of the audience that could not read or had great difficulties in reading subtitles.

---

[1] Usabel (1975, pp. 135–66) presents a detailed account of the various solutions (foreign versions, subtitling, dubbing) undertaken by Hollywood to reach these audiences, and their relative advantages and drawbacks. These "translation" attempts have to be seen in a wider context of U.S. companies' global attempt at penetrating not only Latin America but also all accessible European markets with U.S.-made films spoken in French, German, and Spanish.

Although the arrival of the "talkies" brought new momentum to Argentine and Mexican film production, their paths, relatively similar until 1934, became increasingly divergent after that year. From 1934 on, the state took an entirely different attitude towards local film production in the two countries. In Argentina, the local film industry grew consistently from 1930 to 1939, without any form of state protection. After 1939, however, Argentina's position of neutrality during World War II caused its raw film quota from the United States to be drastically reduced at a time when no other suppliers were available. Unable to supply its Latin American market without celluloid, Argentine film producers concentrated on their domestic market and pressed for protectionist measures. In Mexico, on the other hand, local film production found a receptive atmosphere in government circles preoccupied with the wide diffusion of national integration values across popular social sectors (Turner, 1968, Ch. 7). Furthermore, Mexico's pro-Allies position during the second World War resulted in its film industry being supplied with unlimited quantities of raw film from the U.S., in addition to financial and technical support. State protection and the country's pro-Allies position during the war made possible a process of uninterrupted growth for the Mexican film industry. The following sections present a closer view of both developments.

SOCIETY AND FILM PRODUCTION IN ARGENTINA, 1930–1943

The 1929 international economic crisis had widespread economic and political repercussions in Latin America. In Argentina, President Yrigoyen was deposed by a military coup in September 1930. A conservative coalition headed by Justo soon took power, entailing political arrangements of "limited democracy." International economic conditions, however, prevented the reinstated conservative forces from following their traditional "free trade" economic philosophy. The new Argentine government acknowledged that the international economic crisis impeded the country's economic expansion through foreign markets, and engaged in a moderate program of state-supported industrialization, while the Roca-Runciman treaty signed with England in 1933 assured Argentina of a reduced but stable market for its exports (Peralta Ramos, 1972, p. 77).

Even within a such a framework of mild state support, import-substitution industrialization grew substantially, attracting capital and labor. The 1929 international economic crisis resulted in the interruption of European migration to Argentina. Concurrently, the drastic reduction in the country's agricultural exports produced high unemployment in the countryside. Rural unemployment and state-supported industrialization coincided to produce massive internal migration to urban centers. These new sectors of the urban working classes put increased pressures on urban services and greatly expanded the demand for entertainment. Radio and the local film industry were the mass media that benefited the most.

Sound Film in Argentina, 1931–1943

The first Argentine "talkies" were made in 1930. Technical facilities were extremely precarious, and the overall sound and image quality could hardly compete with that of foreign films. Only by 1933 were local producers able to offer films with acceptable sound. Even though these economic and technical differences created a situation of markedly unequal competition between Argentine and foreign products, other factors would partially offset the foreign advantage and facilitate the development of a local film industry. The popular sectors' illiteracy, the utilization in film of popular radio artists, and film producers' ability to integrate many of the themes and genres developed in popular theatre into local films, favored local film production.

During the 1930s Argentine film production grew consistently, but always in the context of a market dominated by foreign releases (see Tables 3, 4, and 5). Although the large U.S. based companies extended their distribution networks in Argentina, local film production managed to find both a domestic and a Latin American market.[2] By the end of the 1930s some local films began to attract the interest of the middle classes. Some Argentine producers began to aim at the middle-class sector of the audience, a social sector that spent more on entertainment and patronized the best theatres, where Argentine producers hoped to introduce their best products on a "percentage of the gross" basis. (Local films were distributed for flat fees, while foreign distributors could bargain with exhibitors for a percentage of the gross.)

Generally speaking, competition with the large foreign distributors was waged on a very unequal footing because of wide economic, financial, and technical differences. From a technical point of view, for instance, Argentine films did not attain photographic standards similar to those of international productions until 1937. But the most difficult problems were economic, financial, and organizational. Chronic undercapitalization and the need to attract the interest of the middle-class public without losing the patronage of the popular sectors were also aspects of these problems.[3]

[2] In 1931 only four of the U.S. companies maintained branches in cities of the Argentine interior; in 1935 all of them except RKO had established branches in the most important provincial cities (International Motion Pictures Almanac, 1936–1937).

[3] In order to understand the slow capitalization of local film production companies, it should be remembered that even though a few Argentine films appealed to the middle classes, the bulk of the public for local films belonged to a working class with very low wages. Even the most successful Argentine films commanded very low admission prices, and these revenues had to cover both production and distribution costs, while foreign films had only distribution costs to cover.

Although the development of the Argentine film industry was continuous during this decade, some aspects of the industry's mode of operation hindered its chances of making a complete transition toward becoming
a modern industry, and the same structural factors made it vulnerable vis-
à-vis foreign distributors and local exhibitors, in a general context of absence of any type of specific state protection legislation:

1. Absence of a distribution network under local producers' control
   in the provinces.
2. Absence of a reliable distribution network in the Latin American
   market.
3. Other production and distribution problems related to producers'
   chronic under-capitalization (Schnitman, 1979, pp. 69–70).

WORLD WAR II AND
THE ARGENTINE FILM INDUSTRY

After growing continuously during the 1930s, film production in Argentina
suffered pronounced fluctuations throughout the decade of the 1940s
(Table 3). These fluctuations are better understood in the changed international and domestic contexts brought about by World War II.

The war acted as a significant stimulant for the U.S. film industry,
but these bonanza years were based primarily on the domestic market, as
the war had practically closed U.S. film markets in Continental Europe.
This situation enhanced the importance of Latin America as a market for
U.S. films. "To offset conditions in the war-torn European countries,
Hollywood turned to Latin America. There, although the industry had a
near-monopoly, the market had never been fully exploited" (Balio, 1976,
p. 223). Paralleling its renewed economic importance, Latin America acquired an additional politico-ideological importance during the war that
was recognized by the U.S. government.

Coordination of Inter-American Affairs

In October 1940, the United States Department of State created the Office
of the Coordinator of Inter-American Affairs (CIAA), with the objective of
promoting President Roosevelt's Good Neighbor policy and encouraging
initiatives to combat pro-Axis sentiment in Latin America. The CIAA,
under the direction of Nelson Rockefeller, opened a Motion Picture Division headed by Francis Alstock. The creation of this Division was pre-
ceded by a survey of Latin American countries to assess their potential for
film distribution. The survey was conducted by the American Film Center, a consulting agency set up in New York by the Rockefeller Foundation. *Variety* (Dec. 14, 1938, p. 17) reported: "the Center hopes to have [a]

report available for the use of educational, industrial, commercial, and possibly government bodies by the time the Federal Government has its educational good-will program readied." Newsreels were seen as one of the most important vehicles for pro-Allies points of view.

Under President Castillo (1940–1943), Argentina remained neutral, and the United States' attempts to include Argentina in mutual defense agreements and bring the Argentine market under its domination proved to no avail (Daniels, 1970). Some authors (e.g., Scobie, 1971, p. 271) interpreted Argentina's neutrality during the second World War as the result of pressures on the government originated in pro-Axis military groups. Other authors (e.g., Ciria, 1974; Corradi, 1974) pointed out that a neutral Argentina was convenient for both England and Germany. Germany's interest in Argentine neutrality was aimed at protecting German investments there. Britain was concerned that if Argentina joined the Allies, Germany would block the continuous flow of Argentine agricultural products to England. England also expected to keep Argentina within its sphere of influence after the war.

Even though Argentina's neutrality provided food for the British war effort, that neutrality was viewed in U.S. diplomatic circles as outright pro-Axis sympathy.[4] It was feared that some of this alleged pro-Axis ideology could influence the content of Argentine pictures, very popular at the time among Latin American low-income social sectors. The U.S. government concern was based on the fact that some Spanish-speaking films had been made in Germany, and Spain had turned out some pro-Axis films.

Unable to reach all sectors of Latin American spectators with subtitled movies spoken in English, the CIAA decided on a strategy of displacing Argentine films from Latin America, replacing them with films made in a country with firm pro-Allies position, i.e., from Mexico. Towards this end, the Mexican film industry was supported with loans, equipment, technical advice, and a practically unlimited supply of raw film. The Argentine film industry, on the other hand, was allocated a raw film quota from the U.S. insufficient to keep its film production at previous levels. Argentina's technological dependence on this vital element for the film industry made it vulnerable to such a strategy, in a situation where the war made unavailable any film supplies from Europe. From the moment when the effects of this policy were felt in Argentina (in 1940) until the end of the war, all attempts at local manufacture of raw film failed, and processes to recycle used celluloid had very limited success.

---

[4] "War documents recently declassified . . . especially the Churchill-Roosevelt correspondence from 1939 to 1945—reveal that Churchill's reluctance to abide by an economic embargo against the pro-Axis Argentine government was one of the more acrimonious disagreements between the British and the Americans during the War" (Corradi, 1974, p. 359).

In a report from Washington titled "U.S. Still Holding Back on Raw Film Stock to Argentina," *Variety* (July 7, 1943, p. 19) stated:

> No increase in raw film stock shipments to Argentina is foreseen here as the political situation there is regarded as such that alleviation of the squeeze does not appear warranted.... [Argentina's quota] represents about enough footage for 24 films, while some 50 films were produced there last year.

The CIAA attitude towards the Mexican film industry was exactly the reverse. *Variety* (June 30, 1943, p. 25) reported from Mexico City:

> Plans for increasing the scope of existing picture studios and opening of another . . . are being discussed here with Francis Alstock, chief of the film division of the office of the Coordinator of Inter-American Affairs.

From 1943 to the end of World War II, Argentine producers had to work with raw film obtained from their share of the United States quota, or with highly priced black-market stock smuggled into Argentina from neighboring countries. In Buenos Aires, film trade journal *Heraldo del Cine* (March 1, 1944) reported that there could be no royalties from the export of Argentine films due to the unavailability of raw film to make copies.

By 1946, when the first postwar raw film shipments were received from Europe, the position of Argentine films in Latin America was severely reduced; Mexican films had practically replaced them, and would soon receive an extra boost from the organization of Pel-Mex, a state-sponsored distribution company.

From the point of view of U.S.-based interests, the CIAA policy of favoring the Mexican film industry had a double advantage. From an ideological perspective, an Allied country was a better guarantee of suitable motion picture content. From an economic point of view, reducing the importance of the Argentine film industry in Latin America spared American distribution companies a competitor for some fractions of the Latin American markets, and gave U.S. entrepreneurs the opportunity to participate in the development of the Mexican film industry.[5]

[5] By 1945, for instance, RKO owned 49% of the stock of Churubusco film studios, the most important in Mexico in the 1940s. The "Mexicanization" laws prevented RKO, a company to which Rockefeller financial interests were not unrelated, from being Churubusco's sole owners (Sadoul, 1947, vol. 6, p. 248). Columbia Pictures' long standing presence in the production and distribution of Mexican films (Garcia Riera, 1981) provides another example of U.S. companies' participation in the growth of local film production there. See also Mora (1982, pp. 68–69).

After the loss of the Latin American market in the early 1940s, Argentine film producers turned to the state, demanding financial support and a stronger hold on the domestic market. No state support would be forthcoming, however, until 1944, under a government strongly influenced by Perón.

THE ARGENTINE FILM INDUSTRY UNDER PERONISM, 1946–1955

As a member of a provisional military government (1943–1945) and later as President (1946 to 1955), General Perón attempted a process of accelerated, semi-autonomous capitalist development. Perón's government sought to establish a social pact between industrialists and workers under the control of the state. Its overall economic plan included strengthening and streamlining the state protectionist structure to stimulate Argentina's independent industrial development, expand the domestic market, and project Argentine products into Latin America and other foreign markets. The local film industry benefited from general and specific protectionist policies. Under Perón's government state protection measures for the Argentine film industry included:

1944. Compulsory exhibition of Argentine films (screen quota) and distribution on a percentage basis (before 1944 most local films were distributed for flat fees).

1947. Argentine films were given a minimum of 25% of screen time in the best Buenos Aires theatres, and 40% of screen time in the rest of the country, a distinction that reflected the more cosmopolitan taste of the middle and upper-class audiences that attended the first-run theatres located in the capital.

1948. The Industrial Bank granted special loans for local film production; bilateral pacts for film exchange were signed; a film production subsidy funded through a new admissions tax was established.

By 1948, however, the results of unplanned state protection, or state protection that was not part of a general cultural policy, were still unclear. Screen quotas, bank loans, and production subsidies determined a quantitative growth in local film production, but the number of unimportant films ("quota quickies") also increased. Furthermore, while in 1948 more local films were exported to the Latin American market, producers continued operating separately and sold their products for flat fees. Also in 1948, at the producer's request, the Argentine government attempted to implement its most advanced measure in the area of international film policy—a reciprocity system with the countries that exported their films to Argentina. This reciprocity policy was consistent with the Perón government's attempt to save hard currency; the broad project was to conduct as much as possible of Argentina's international trade through bilateral pacts. In other words, Argentina would buy the products of the countries that bought Argentine products.

The Argentine bilateral economic policy had different effects on the country's film relations with various countries. Successful film exchanges were conducted with Spain, Italy, France, and Czechoslovakia. But for the companies represented by the Motion Picture Export Association of America (MPEA), the Argentine government insistence on reciprocity and foreign exchange controls was unacceptable. MPEA's objectives in the Argentine market were the same as in any other market of the world: free trade. Free trade meant freedom to introduce U.S. pictures in the Argentine market in a quantity limited only by market receptivity, and the possibility to convert into dollars and remit to companies' headquarters the revenues received in local currency. U.S. film companies and the MPEA did not accept Argentina's reciprocity policy.

The Johnston-Cereijo Agreement

The MPEA did not accept the Argentine government reciprocity demands, and by the end of 1948 Argentine authorities suspended the issuance of import permits for U.S. films. The large American film companies operated during 1949 and 1950 by re-releasing popular old films, liberating a considerable portion of screen time for European, Mexican, and local productions (Table 6).

The predicament of the large American companies in Argentina during this stage of the Peronist administration was not only a result of a specific policy toward film but also a result of general restrictions on the funds that all foreign companies in Argentina could send to their headquarters. These restrictions were based on a hard currency scarcity and the industralization projects of the Argentine government. All companies, foreign and domestic, were expected to reinvest a substantial part of their earnings in Argentina. The 1950 foreign currency scarcity was further aggravated in 1951 by a drought, and a decline in the international prices for Argentine agricultural products.

The foreign currency scarcity situation prompted a change in the economic policy of the Peronist government; the new economic policy included a more receptive attitude toward foreign companies operating or willing to operate in Argentina, and a general revision of the terms of U.S.-Argentina relations. In the specific field of film, a pact was signed in Washington, D.C. on May 12, 1950, between Johnston, head of the MPEA, and

Cereijo, the Argentine Minister of Finance. The agreement was similar to other documents signed after World War II between the MPEA (with the assistance of the U.S. State Department) and some Western European countries that were experiencing foreign currency shortages.

Variety (May 17, 1950, p. 12) reported that the State Department was actively helping American companies to negotiate an agreement with both England and Argentina. In this latter case the "part that the State Department played. . .is understood to have been far more active [than with England]. It expressed itself as extremely anxious that a deal be made as part of a general policy of getting friendly with the Argentines." Variety stated that the State Department had recently approved a $125 million loan to the Argentine government, and this loan was the element opening the door to the U.S.-Argentina agreement in the area of film.

The Johnston-Cereijo pact granted the American companies represented by the MPEA remittances from Argentina to headquarters of over five million dollars in a five-year period. Considering both frozen funds and future earnings, this amounted to approximately one-third of American distributors earnings in the Argentine market. The terms of the agreement included a guarantee that U.S. film companies would be allowed to remit dividends on their investments if other foreign industries were granted similar privileges, a move considered highly probable as part of the new policy towards foreign capital. The Johnston-Cereijo pact was not operative until the beginning of 1952, resulting in a three-year lag (1949–1951) in the flow of Hollywood pictures to the Argentine market.

Increased Protectionism in Argentina

The two years preceding the signing of the Johnston-Cereijo agreement (1949 and 1950) saw a drastic reduction in the flow of Hollywood pictures to the Argentine market, and this reduction liberated more screen time for domestic productions. After the pact was signed, Variety (June 7, 1950, p. 15) reported that in Buenos Aires "local film producers are rushing out their productions, ready to skim all the cream they can before the North American pic[tures] start competing again".

Many sectors of the Argentine middle-class public, however, preferred to watch old film reissues or other forms of entertainment. Theatre attendance declined by 30% in 1950. This decline in attendance and the weak position of Argentine films in the Latin American market created a new crisis for Argentine film production. The solution sought and obtained took the form of stiffer protectionist measures. Local producers benefited from both an increase in their participation in theatres' gross revenues and a reduction in "hold-over" (average number of weekly spectators that a picture must attract in order to be shown for another week in the same theatre).

The increase in state protection, however, could not easily offset the crisis of an industry deprived both of a consistent external market and a supportive middle class public. The Argentine film industry was also limited by censorship in its treatment of social and other issues, and was besieged in its domestic market by the renewed presence of Hollywood films, and by the incipient but nonetheless perceptible inroads of television, inaugurated in 1950.

In connection with the marketing of films in Latin America, the government announced in September 1950, that it was prepared to create a joint private-state company to distribute domestic films abroad. This project followed the line of action undertaken by Mexico many years before. The Argentine state-sponsored foreign distribution company, however, never went beyond the planning stage. Authorities acknowledged the critical situation of the Argentine film industry, but the inherent limitations of their cultural policies prevented them from finding ways to improve the situation. Apold, Undersecretary of Difussion, stated in 1951: "It would seem that state protection has only stimulated a quantitative but not a qualitative improvement in films" (quoted in Mahieu, 1974, p. 55).

The number of Argentine films released decreased from 56 in 1950 to 35 in 1952 (a 38% decline), and remained relatively low in 1953 when 37 films were made (Table 3). New factors help to account for these fluctuations in output: The resumption of the significant presence of American pictures in the Argentine domestic market after the signing of the 1950 agreement,[6] television inroads, and the government policy of keeping admission prices low. For local producers, the only way to partially offset these factors was to demand a larger share of gross revenues and more generous subsidies.

The Argentine film industry's new crisis in 1952 was reflected in the bankruptcy of a large company, while two other middle-size companies closed down, and many independents stopped production. Several Argentine directors made plans to work in Chile. Lacking general guidelines for the reorganization of the film industry, the government resorted to a new increase in state protection. Amidst the protectionist policies and measures of the 1949–1955 period, the absence of a general communication policy with well-defined objectives and carefully planned procedures stands out. In general, state protectionism in Argentina determined a quantitative

---

[6] After the signing of the 1950 Johnston-Cereijo agreement, the position of American films in the Argentine market strengthened again. In 1954, for instance, 234 U.S. films were released in Argentina, or 63% of all films released (Table 8). American distributors participated in the release of 247 pictures (Table 7). Since this number is larger than the number of films of U.S. origins (Table 8), it can be inferred that American companies were distributing films made in Europe in Latin America, a trend that would become more important later. Fox, for instance, was distributing French films in Latin America by 1955, and was also looking forward to being in charge of Italian material (*Heraldo del Cine,* May 11, 1955).

growth in local film production, but coupled with censorship, and certain problems built into the subsidy system itself, it favored a certain proliferation of undistinguished films (Mahieu, 1974, p. 51). The Peronist government's inability to devise innovative approaches to the problems of local film production can be attributed both to the inherent limitations of a populist government bent on enlarging the domestic market without affecting the basic mechanisms of a market economy, and to the increasingly difficult political crises that Perón and his government faced from 1952 on.

Between 1950 and 1952 the Peronist project of relatively independent industrialization reached its limits, showing that it was a program heavily dependent upon the country's ability to export. If before 1930 Argentine imports concentrated on finished products, the subsequent industrialization process changed the type of goods imported but did not alter the country's dependence on foreign suppliers. Instead of finished products, import-substitution industrialization entailed the importation of heavy machinery, advanced technology, and some raw materials.

The depletion of the hard currency surplus accumulated during World War II set the stage for the demise of Peronism. The Peronist government was forced to choose between the differing interests of the two classes that had provided its social base; it was no longer possible to satisfy both the working class demands for higher real wages and the capital-technological needs of the industrial bourgeoisie.

By 1952 governmental policies were fully reoriented toward the needs of the industrial bourgeoisie, and a more open attitude toward foreign investment was introduced to reactivate the level of economic activity. In these post-war years, the United States was the only country able to supply Argentina with both capital and technology. The first signs of a new Peronist attitude toward U.S. capital occurred in 1950, when the Argentine government guaranteed a 125 million dollar loan granted by the Export-Import Bank for the Importation of American products. Meat packing, petroleum, and other U.S. industries were allowed to invest in Argentina. It was at this moment that the 1950 pact reopening the doors to American distributors was signed. A new law passed in 1953 opened new areas to foreign investment, but still set precise limits to its expansion.[7]

Around 1954 the political scene witnessed a realignment of forces. The landed upper-classes, always against the Peronist government, were joined in their opposition by the church, sectors of the army, and important sectors of the industrial bourgeoisie. Industrialists wanted a more open policy toward foreign sources of capital and technology, and expected

[7] The government's turn toward foreign capital determined that "American and West European firms began taking over major sectors of Argentine industry. With tariff protection now working in their favor, American, German, and Italian firms developed high-cost automobile plants and chemical complexes" (Corradi, 1974, p. 373).

a stronger anti-labor policy, a course of action that Perón was reluctant to
to follow. By 1955, when the military coup that finally overthrew Peron
took place, the industrial sector was no longer a supporter of the government.

STATE POLICIES TOWARD FILM
IN ARGENTINA, 1955–1980

The government in power after the military coup of September 1955,
adopted as one of its policies the dismantling of the Peronist government
protectionist structure for the local film industry. The new authorities
lifted all restrictions on the introduction of foreign films in the domestic
market and announced that foreign distributors' earnings could be freely
remitted abroad.[8]

After the military coup that removed Perón from office in September
1955, the Argentine state policies towards local film production changed
drastically, reflecting the important changes that took place in other areas
of economic, social, and cultural policy. The state protectionist structure
benefiting local industries was dismantled, and foreign capital was again
allowed to operate in Argentina under reduced controls. All restrictions to
the importation of foreign films were lifted, creating an overabundance of
foreign productions in the domestic market that proved overpowering for
local producers. After some delay, and following considerable pressure
from groups concerned with local production, a new protectionist scheme
for the local film industry was announced by the government in 1957.

The new protectionist system involved the creation of a National
Film Institute, production loans, a government subsidy, and prizes for
quality films. The breakdown of the protectionist system after the fall of
Peronism in 1955 accounts for the final decline of the studio system in
Argentina. After 1957 all local production was undertaken on a film-by-
film basis.

A new attempt to regulate the flow of foreign films was made in 1962.
The National Film Institute proposed a "six for one" formula: Six foreign
films were to be allowed in Argentina in proportion to each local film released. It was thought that this measure would stimulate local production,
and induce foreign producers to invest in local production. In 1963 the

---

[8] A similar trend was apparent in other mass media. The new political situation made possible
the introduction into Argentina of dubbed American television series: "It is pointed out in
New York that under the previous [Perón] government Argentine television was closed not
only to the American entertainment material but also to the American-based international
advertising companies and their clients, the international divisions of many large American
corporations" (*Heraldo del Cine*, Nov. 2, 1955).

project was formalized into a law that, for the first time in the history of Argentine film protection legislation, made all distributors operating in the country responsible for marketing at least one Argentine picture for each group of six foreign films they released in the domestic market. Distributors staunchly opposed this new legislation, and the whole project was abandoned after Eric Johnston, head of the Motion Picture Export Association, visited Argentina (Mahieu, 1974, p. 80). A few years before, Johnston had stated that, in view of the fact that U.S. films filled a large proportion of foreign countries' screen time, if any of these countries wanted to restrict the flow of American films, he could "go to the Finance Minister [of the country in question]. . . to simply state that our films keep more than half of the theatres open. This means employment and a bolstering factor for the economy of whichever country is involved. And I can tell the Finance Minister of the tax revenue which these theatres yield" (*Variety*, Oct. 10, 1956, p. 11).

Further revisions of the protectionist structure for the local film industry were introduced by subsequent governments. All the protectionist systems implemented after 1955, however, failed to effect a sustained new growth in local film production. Under the conditions of (1) competition with foreign film industries that reduces the potential domestic market, (2) local exhibitors organized into chains, (3) higher production costs, (4) competition with television, and (5) censorship that questions, in local films, the treatment of social, political, and other themes tolerated in foreign films, the Argentine film industry would not know another growth period. It remained at a level of an average of 30 productions per year between 1956 and 1981, while film production in Mexico averaged 71 pictures per year in the same period. The following sections concentrate on the events that gave that definite competitive edge to Mexican film production.

FILM INDUSTRY IN MEXICO IN THE 1930s

The advent of sound gave Mexican film producers a new opportunity to reach their domestic audiences and other audiences throughout Latin America. The role of the state in aiding this process was far more important in Mexico than in Argentina.[9] In 1934 the state guaranteed a loan to finance the construction of the first modern film studio in Mexico City.

[9] Anderson and Cockcroft (1972, p. 222) identified the following "goal structure" of the Mexican political system after the Mexican Revolution. Their characterization clarifies the background for the Mexican state's behavior toward the country's film industry: a. Political stability; b. Economic growth, through industrialization and modernization of agriculture; c. Public welfare; and d. Mexicanization, or the policy of securing control over major economic companies and activities in the country for both private Mexican citizens and public agencies.

State ministries financed the production of two feature films, and plans were underway to create a complex system of film production financing organized by the Secretary of Public Education (Garcia Riera, 1969, vol. 1, p. 69).[10]

Two positions of state policy towards the local film industry competed in Mexico during the early 1930s: film as a centralized and nationalized industry, and film as a private industry undertaken by a variety of small firms. By 1936, when the civil war in Spain hindered film production there and reduced competition for Mexican film production, advocacy of a privately owned Mexican film industry prevailed. Overall, however, and with various emphases in different historical circumstances, the role of the state in local film production, and later on in film distribution and exhibition, favored a unique combination of the two organizational philosophies. In time, the net result was a local film industry combining state and privately owned production, distribution, and exhibition facilities.

The government of President Cárdenas (1934–1940) took an active interest in the development of the Mexican film industry, in a general context of economic and social policies aimed at boosting the country's industrialization process and strengthening the state's intervention in the economy to cope with the international economic depression. These policies included agrarian reform, nationalization of the oil industry, rural and urban labor codes, and state investment in the industrial sector.[11] Under President Cárdenas the Mexican state developed a protectionist policy for domestic film production that included: a. Tax exemptions for the local film industry; b. Creation of a state institution (Financiadora de Peliculas) to provide loans for film production; and, c. Loans for the building of studios. In October 1939, Cárdenas issued a decree that made it mandatory for all Mexican theatres to show at least one domestic film each month. After Cárdenas, President Avila Camacho (1941–1946) continued and extended the protectionist system for the local film industry. Generally speaking, the political continuity afforded by the continuous rule of the majority party in Mexico created a better context for a consistent protectionist policy for the local film industry than the socio-political discontinuities of Argentina's contemporary history.

[10] Precedents for the Mexican state interest in both the educational possibilities of film and a comprehensive national film policy are found as early as the beginning of the 1920s (Usabel, 1975, pp. 77–78).

[11] Available evidence indicates that, despite the revolutionary language of the Cárdenas government, it did not preside over a transition from capitalism to socialism but over a continuing model of capitalist industrial growth, modernization of the agricultural sector, and the preservation of private property and the various foreign and domestic private interests within a framework of state assistance and regulation (Cockcroft, 1974, p. 261). (For a detailed study of the context and limits of the Mexican state intervention in the economy under Cárdenas, see Hamilton (1982).)

In this period, several forms of state support favored the remarkable expansion of local film production in Mexico. From 1941 to 1946 President Avila Camacho continued and expanded the protectionist policy for the national film industry inaugurated by Cárdenas. The government ratified and enforced the mandatory exhibition of Mexican films in all Mexican theatres, and a Film Bank was created in 1942 to modernize and expand the activities previously undertaken by Financiadora de Peliculas. The creation of the Film Bank, a private institution strongly supported by the Mexican state, was "the most important expression of state support for the Mexican film industry" (Garcia Riera, 1969, vol. II, p. 53). The Film Bank supported the creation of a large production and distribution company integrated with most of the larger local firms engaged in film production and distribution, thus effecting a combine that Mexican private capital had been unable or unwilling to accomplish on its own. By 1943, the preeminence of the Mexican film industry in Latin America was an established fact, made possible in part by the continuous support from the U.S. during World War II, and by the reorganization of film production and distribution through the newly created Film Bank (Heuer, 1964, p. 17).

After World War II film production in Mexico went through a transition period reflected in a quantitative decline in 1946 and 1947 (Table 3), but this circumstance was offset by a reorganization and expansion of the state protectionist system. The Film Bank, created in 1942 as a private institution with state participation, was transformed in 1947 into a National Film Bank under full state control. The National Film Bank supported the creation of three distribution companies to organize the domestic and foreign distribution of all Mexican films. The Latin American film market was of the utmost importance for the Mexican film industry, and some years later a former Director of the National Film Bank wrote that Pel-Mex, the state enterprise in charge of film distribution in Latin America, was probably the best established Mexican enterprise and with the most ramifications abroad (Heuer, 1964, p. 43). This reorganization of the state protectionist system accounts for a new growth in quantitative output that continued until the early 1960s (Table 3).

From a cultural point of view, however, from 1945 on the high levels of state protection and the "closed doors" policy followed by the Film Production Workers Union (that included film directors) seems to have had a stultifying effect on creativity, thematic diversity, and film directors' eagerness to include critical views in their films. Two critics have expressed the view that "the same directors, the same actors, made the same scripts, written by the same script-writers, utilizing the same cinematographers, in films designed for the same potential audience formed by millions of Latin American illiterates. . . while producers tried to make as much money as possible to be reinvested in safer enterprises" (Torres and Perez Estremera, 1973, p. 178).

STATE PROTECTIONISM AND FILM INDUSTRY IN MEXICO AFTER THE LATE 1950s

During the 1960s and 1970s the Mexican state continued expanding its participation in all aspects of local film production, distribution, and exhibition. Overall, however, such state participation has not resulted in a definitive nationalization or statization of film production, but in a support system either for local entrepreneurs, or for film industry workers, or both. Mexican economists Aguilar and Carmona, paraphrasing a Mexican banker, have described the private sector's perception of the Mexican state' general economic role as follows: "it is the duty of the state humbly to set the table, and the job of private enterprise to eat what it finds there" (Aguilar and Carmona, 1967, p. 65). Churubusco, Mexico's leading studios and laboratories, were purchased by the state in 1959, and the principal domestic exhibition chain of theatres, Operadora de Teatros, was nationalized in 1960. While, in the early 1960s Mexican state participation in all aspects of the local film industry was estimated at 50% (Heuer, 1964, p. 93), a few years later the National Film Bank generated 90% of all financing for local film, and coordinated companies involved in filmmaking, distribution, exhibition, and promotion (Perez Turrent and Turner, 1976, p. 208). By the early 1970s the state owned 60% of all Mexican theatres, with the company distributing 95% of locally-made films.

Beginning in 1970, and due to lack of interest on the part of private producers, the National Film Bank began acting as a direct producer, sometimes in association with film technicians and workers. Following the same trend of greater state intervention and protection, in 1975 the state purchased the America studios, the second-best in the country after the state-owned Churubusco, and created two new state production companies. A more recent trend, dating from about 1977, indicates a return to activity of some private producers, still within a framework of clear state hegemony in the process of local film financing, distribution, and exhibition. By the end of 1978, the National Film Bank, head of the state protectionist system, was integrated into the Directorate of Radio, Television, and Cinema (DRTC), a new structure designed to function as a Ministry of Communications, in charge of all communications policies in Mexico (Perez Turrent and Turner, 1979). One year later the Film Bank was formally dissolved (Mora, 1982, p. 138).

The above changes were related to the change in the political climate brought about by the government of López Portillo (1976–1982), that favored the return of private film producers, and the further incursions of Televisa, the giant private television company, into the production of films starring popular TV figures.[12]

The most innovative solutions to the quantitative decline in film production were taken during President Echeverría's government (1970–1976): film workers' participation in film production, the organization of fully state-owned film production companies, and a liberalization of censorship.[13] Overall, the fluctuating participation of the state in the various facets of the domestic film process has resulted in a relatively high yearly output of local films (Table 3). The Mexican state action has also resulted in a sustained source of work for Mexican film workers, technicians, and actors, has ensured that the main mechanisms of the industry have remained under local state or private control (as per the Mexicanization laws), and has generated profits for local entrepreneurs.

Although state participation in the Mexican film industry can be viewed as a complex and variable interaction of economic, political, and ideological components (of which film industry workers' pressures and the Mexican state legitimacy needs are also aspects), from a strictly economic perspective, state action appears to have functioned to ensure the socialization of the industry's deficits and the privatization of its profits[14] (Sanchez, 1981, passim. especially pp. 47–48 and 63–64).

FILM INDUSTRIES AND STATE PROTECTION IN ARGENTINA AND MEXICO: AN OVERVIEW

The scope of state protectionism in Argentina, although increasing constantly from 1944 to 1955, was never as far-reaching and efficient as the

[12] "López Portillo named his sister, Margarita López Portillo, as head of the Directorate of Radio, Television, and Cinema (DRTC), a newly formed agency for the coordination of all government-owned production activities in the electronic mass media. As regarded the film industry, this was the first step in the implementation of Lopez Portillo's overall economic program to encourage private enterprise and discard government-owned enterprises...In the movie industry this meant the retreat of the State from direct participation in filmmaking and the return of private producers" (Mora, 1982, pp. 137–38).

[13] Sanchez, however, presents a complex argument extremely critical of state film policies and the films made during the Echeverría sexenio (Sanchez, 1981, passim, especially Chapter 4).

[14] It is also possible to claim that this is the main function of most cases of state intervention in the economy in all social formations both at the center and in the periphery of the capitalist world system. Hamilton (1982) presents an exhaustive theoretical and historical study of the possibilities and limits to state autonomy and state intervention in the economy in post-revolutionary Mexico. Her conclusions, however, have implications that go well beyond the Mexican case.

Mexican state protectionist system. The Argentine state never intervened directly in the areas of film distribution and exhibition (never acquired facilities in these areas), and plans to create UniArgentina, the equivalent of Pel-Mex, a state enterprise in charge of distributing national films abroad, were never implemented. The continuous increase in state protection could not offset the situation of a local film industry without a consistent external market, and without a supportive middle class public at home. The Argentine film industry was also limited by censorship in its treatment of social, political, and moral issues, and was besieged in its own domestic market by foreign films, and by television from 1950 on.

In brief, even though under Peronism (1944–1955), state protectionism for the local film industry experienced a continuous increase, its measures were never as far-reaching as the ones undertaken by the Mexican state, and could not completely offset the domestic and foreign factors that, coupled with censorship and a non-supportive middle-class audience, determined an indecisive course for the Argentine film industry. In Argentina, the first protectionist measures were taken in 1944. In Mexico, state protectionism for the local film industry came ten years earlier, and grew to include aspects of the activity never considered in the Argentine protectionist system (i.e., distribution and domestic and foreign exhibition). These factors, plus the all-important U.S. support during World War II, gave a clear advantage to the Mexican film industry. After the war state protectionism continued to be much more effective and encompassing in Mexico than in Argentina.

STATE PROTECTIONISM AND FILM INDUSTRY DEVELOPMENT

This presentation of the major trends in state protectionism for the respective film industries in Argentina and Mexico makes it apparent that the choice and implementation of protectionist measures for local mass media industries in developing countries is not a simple process of social engineering. Either as a set of specific political measures, or as part of general communication policies, protectionism originates in a complex socio-economic, political, and cultural context. Derived from such a broad context, protectionist measures, in turn, interact with and influence at least some aspects of their context. The final effects of protectionist measures will depend in part on the design and implementation of the measures themselves, and also on their interaction with other significant elements of the economic, political, and cultural environment of the society in question, and of other significant actors in the world system.

The general trend of state protectionism in Argentina was and still is geared to keeping all initiative in the private sector. After the virtual loss of their Latin American markets during World War II, local producers received considerable assistance from the state, in the context of a govern-ment committed to supporting the expansion of all domestic industrial production (Perón, 1944–1955). This period was followed by a phase of complete "laissez faire" (1955–1977), with an overwhelming importation of foreign films, and then by a period of rather moderate and sometimes laxly implemented protectionism (1977–present).

In Mexico, on the other hand, the general trend has been towards more decisive participation of the state in all phases of local film produc-tion, distribution (including foreign distribution), and exhibition, com-plementing and even replacing private entrepreneurs when necessary, although it should be remembered that state protectionism in Mexico operates within a general context of private property. State intervention in local film activities in Mexico was intended to facilitate the activities of local entrepreneurs and sometimes, exceptionally, of film workers, suc-ceeding in many cases to unify most of the interests involved through the ideological dynamism of Mexican nationalism as a unifying politico-cul-tural force (Turner, 1968, Ch. 1).

While the role of the state in the development of a local film industry grew almost continuously in Mexico, in Argentina it was remarkably dis-continuous, paralleling the discontinuities in the Argentine political process, in the same fashion as the evolution of Mexican protectionism paralleled the basic continuity in the Mexican political process.

This comparative analysis has highlighted the importance of state protectionism for the survival and growth of mass communication indus-tries in developing countries. The question then arises about the most effective forms of state support for local mass media industries. In the case of film, a distinction between *restrictive* and *supportive* protectionist poli-cies can be suggested.

A purely *restrictive* state protectionist policy would concentrate on measures designed to impede a complete take-over of the domestic film market by foreign products by means of screen quotas, import quotas, high import taxes, and other measures. A *supportive* state protectionist policy would concentrate on various forms of direct support for the local film industry through bank loans, production subsidies, organization of a foreign distribution service for local films, scholarships and fellowships for film technicians, etc. A *comprehensive* state protectionist policy would include both restrictive (of foreign competition) and supportive (of domes-tic film production) aspects.

In Western Europe restrictive protectionism took two basic forms: screen quotas and foreign films quotas. The screen quota system sets apart a portion of each theatre's screen time for domestic films, while the for-eign film quota sets a limit on the number of foreign films imported each year. Supportive protectionism followed three main procedures: prizes, loans, and subsidies. Prizes are awarded to films on the basis of their merit; loans and credits often involve the creation of a special bank, while in general the state subsidy returns to producers a certain proportion of a tax paid by the public on the theatres' admission price (see Guback, 1969, passim).

Both Argentina and Mexico have used screen quotas as the single most important restrictive protectionist measure, although import quotas have also been enforced under certain circumstances. It is the extent of the supportive measures that has been remarkably different. Brazil, on the other hand, has relied almost exclusively on an ever increasing screen quota; sustained direct state support measures are relatively recent. The next chapter concentrates on film production and state policies in Brazil, a country that shares with Argentina and Mexico a reliance on a large domestic market.

Chapter 5

Society and the Film Industry in Brazil, 1930–1980[1]

The preceding chapter introduced the notions of supportive, restrictive, and comprehensive state protectionism. Like most typologies, this one makes relative, more than absolute, distinctions. In Brazil, for instance, screen quotas, i.e., the policy of reserving a certain amount of screen time for local productions, have been the main instrument of state support for local film production. Screen quotas can be seen as supportive of local film production and only *indirectly* restrictive of imports. As in other Latin American countries, the content and implementation of this and other protectionist measures in Brazil varied widely depending upon the general socioeconomic and political context, and the changed importance of film as a mass medium after the advent of television.

As stated in Chapter 2, during the era of silent films Brazilian film production grew only under the exceptional circumstances of a short-lived vertical integration of national entrepreneurs (between 1908 and 1911), and made a faint attempt at recovery when World War I created a virtual elimination of imported European films. No state protection for local film production was available during the era of silent films.

Most large U.S.-based companies opened their Brazilian branches at this time, benefiting both from the interruption in the flow of European pictures and the transition toward distribution based on film rentals. Para-

[1] I am indebted to Burns (1980), Dos Santos (1974), and Keen and Wasserman (1980) as sources for the socioeconomic and political history of Brazil. Unless otherwise noted, sources for the history of film production and state protectionism in Brazil are Gonzaga and Salles Gomes (1966), Johnson (1982a, 1982b), Paranagua (1981), and Santos Pereira (1973).

mount inaugurated its Brazilian branch in 1916, Universal in 1917, followed by Warner Bros. and United Artists. By 1924, the predominance of U.S. films in the Brazilian market paralleled a similar phenomenon in the rest of Latin America: 1,477 films (features and shorts) were presented for censorship in Rio de Janeiro, of which 1,268 (86%) originated in the U.S. (Santos Pereira, 1973, p. 229).

Unable to secure more than a marginal role in its own domestic market, Brazilian film production languished throughout the 1920s, cornered by a massive influx of foreign films that reinforced a pre-industrial mode of production. Local films continued to be made through producers' and directors' personal efforts.

STATE POLICY AND FILM PRODUCTION IN BRAZIL 1930–1950: ESTADO NOVO AND POPULISM

At the beginning of the 1930s local film production in Brazil had opportunities and problems similar to those found in Argentina and Mexico. There was a vast potential to supply the domestic market with films spoken in Portuguese, but no protectionist system was operative to help local film production during its infancy with the new technology. Even though the transition toward sound films coincided with the inauguration of the Vargas government and a favorable government attitude toward import-substitution industrialization, the Vargas government's measures in the area of film were insufficient to foster local production of a magnitude comparable to the one attained spontaneously in Argentina and under mild state protectionism in Mexico.

Vargas' accession to power coincided with the boom of the "talkies." Sound technicians from the U.S., France, and Germany competed for the installment and maintenance of sound equipment, and by the summer of 1930 Brazilian exhibitors had acquired 165 German and 52 American sound projectors. Brazilian equipment made in cooperation with an American company was also successful (Usabel, 1975, p. 353). With the advent of sound, Paramount, MGM, and local entrepreneurs began to build more theatres in the principal cities, and more films were imported. American film maintained its clear hegemony: 81.7% of the 1,200 features and shorts exhibited in Brazil in 1934 were from the U.S. (Variety, Feb. 26, 1936, p. 22).

For local film producers, the 1930s began with renewed enthusiasm and increased production. Very soon, however, the hard realities of economic crisis, political instability, and the unlimited importation of foreign films coincided to cause a drastic reduction in local film production (Table 3). Such a context was hardly conducive to helping local film production face the challenges of the new technology, the result being that an average of only 7 features per year were made between 1934 and 1939.

The world crisis of 1929 had had a deep effect on Brazil's economic and political patterns. Between 1929 and 1931 the international price of coffee dropped sharply; Brazil's foreign trade fell 37% by volume and 67% in value (Burns, 1980, p. 395). By the end of 1930 the country's gold reserves were exhausted. It should also be remembered that by 1930 the United States had already replaced England as Brazil's main trading partner, providing both loans and manufactured products. The presidential campaign and election of 1930 took place in a context of economic crisis that exacerbated traditional class and regional conflicts. Preexistent conflicts between large coffee growers partial to "freedom of commerce" policies, and urban middle sectors interested in furthering industrialization came into sharper focus. These conflicts were reflected in the two coalitions that confronted each other in the 1930 presidential election. One coalition represented coffee planters from São Paulo, their rural allies in other states, and the commercial sectors engaged in the import-export trade. The other coalition (the Liberal Alliance) included the bulk of the urban groups and landowners from states that resented São Paulo's dominant position. Getulio Vargas, whose presence would remain central in Brazilian politics until his death in 1954, was the candidate of the latter coalition.

Vargas' program called for the promotion of industry, the implementation of social welfare legislation, reforms in the political, educational, and juridical systems, and even some moderate reforms in rural areas. Defeated in elections widely considered fraudulent, Vargas was nonetheless installed by the military as president of a provisional government. Such a move signalled the death of the Old Republic, born in 1889 and dominated by the coffee oligarchy. Import-substitution industrialization would be the new motto.

Vargas steered a middle course between the interests of coffee growers and urban middle sectors, encouraging further advances in industrialization as a means toward a dynamization of the economy based on the expansion of the domestic market. The industrialization process, aided by the loss of import capacity, received new impetus from such Vargas policies as exchange control, import quotas, tax incentives for local industrial production, and long term loans at low interest rates. As a result industrial production doubled between 1931 and 1936.

A new constitution, promulgated in 1934, strengthened the powers of the executive, and established that the president was to serve for four years and could not succeed himself. Vargas was elected president for a term that would extend to January 1938. The new constitution stressed the government's role in the country's economic development, and included a section on the rights and duties of labor, reflecting the growing importance of the working class, itself an important part of the potential and actual audience for local film productions.

While the Vargas government favored and protected most other consumer industries, it showed a comparative neglect of local film production. Data indicate (Table 3) that in the early 1930s Brazilian film producers were having much more difficulty securing a foothold in their own domestic market than their colleagues in either Argentina or Mexico. To face such a situation, both film producers and technicians organized their first professional associations, and their first National Film Congress met in Rio de Janeiro in 1932. The demands of this congress concentrated mostly on "supportive" protectionism: compulsory exhibition of Brazilian films, and tariff reductions for the importation of equipment and raw film stock. No import quotas for foreign films were mentioned. It has been pointed out that film producers' industrial outlook at the time was more backward than that of other industrialists (Bernardet, 1979, Chs. 1 and 2). Brazilian film producers maintained little communication with other industrial sectors, and the advanced industrial groups showed little interest in films as a national industry.

At this stage of their development, Brazilian film producers and directors interpreted the typical bottlenecks in film distribution and exhibition as production problems. Better local productions were thought to be needed to compete with imported films; a fully developed structure of industrial film production was thought to be the solution. But while a Hollywood-like production structure was the dream (Galvao, 1982) its implementation in Brazil, a capitalist dependent country, would prove problematic time and again.

The Vargas government enacted a decree in April 1932, establishing that all foreign pictures released in Brazil should be accompanied by a locally produced short ("national complement"). It is interesting to note that the same decree drastically reduced the import tariffs on foreign films. The background for the 1932 decree was not only the government intention of both supporting and controlling local film production, but also the fact that film attendance, hard hit by the international economic depression, had dropped to 40% less than in 1930, while foreign distributors found it very difficult to purchase dollars to remit to headquarters. Vargas' managing to facilitate the importation of foreign (mostly U.S.) films through lower tariffs and establish a moderate degree of state protection for local filmmaking all in the same decree is an excellent example of the conciliation course that he would follow in many other problems confronting his government. In any case, the 1932 decree pioneered the policy of establishing something of a screen quota for local film production. At this stage of their development state protectionism and government control went hand in hand, as overseeing the application of this decree was entrusted to a Federal Censorship Commission under the Ministry of Education.

The 1932 decree instituting the mandatory exhibition of Brazilian shorts favored a proliferation of small production companies that survived mostly through the production of short documentaries and newsreels geared to present a favorable view of government action. These productions' quality, judged very low by contemporary observers, improved after 1935 when the government offered cash prizes for the best productions.

As Paranagua noted (1981, p. 123), the state attitude towards local film production was a complex one, integrating centralization and control, some concessions to national production groups, and attempts at political instrumentalization of the medium. This political influence and control became more direct a few years later when the government propaganda agency began to produce its own documentaries and newsreels that filled the "national complement" quota.

Even though the main thrust of the Vargas 1932 decree and a complementary 1934 decree favored the importation of U.S. films, the 1935 report by the Chief of the Motion Pictures Section, U.S. Department of Commerce, made clear that U.S. interests resented the limited support that the "national complement" provisions represented for Brazilian film production (*Film Daily Yearbook*, 1935, p. 1015). U.S. interests in the area of film were reassured when the 1935 U.S.-Brazil Commercial Treaty specifically forbade the imposition of foreign film import quotas. This was another early instance of U.S.-based companies power to lobby in favor of their interests at very high government levels. Such U.S. lobbying became a continuous feature of negotiations whenever Brazilian interests mobilized in favor of more adequate state protection.

Brazilian filmmakers had neither a global contextual understanding of their activity nor enough political weight to oppose the U.S.-Brazil Commercial Treaty of 1935. Not until 20 years later, with the commercial failure of the Vera Cruz company in São Paulo in 1954, would Brazilian filmmakers begin to consider the situation of Brazilian cinema as part of a global national and international structure.

Film Production In Brazil, 1930–1945

From 1933 to 1949 the production of feature films was concentrated in Rio de Janeiro. This production (Table 3) was much weaker than in either Argentina or Mexico, pointing to both the lack of any external market and a very weak domestic market.

Throughout the 1930s Cinedia and Carmen Santos' Brasil Vita Filmes were the most important production companies, and they made the first attempts at industrial film production. In the process of transition from silent to sound films, some Brazilian directors had worked in Hollywood's "foreign versions," a training ground for many Latin American directors interested in the new technology. One of these, Adhémar Gonzaga, founded Cinedia in 1930. Although overall investments were modest[2] Cinedia was equipped with four sets of sound equipment, a large studio, and two laboratories (Uṣabel, 1975, p. 356). Cinedia averaged two films per year between 1930 and 1945, reaching a high mark of five productions in 1936. Brasil Vita Filmes produced only 13 films between its founding in 1933 and 1958.

After attempting to compete with Hollywood through dramas and other "serious" films, the musical revue proved the most successful genre, a genre that, as in the case of Argentina, allowed for an alliance with another powerful mass medium and its artists, the radio. The musical comedy and its subsequent transmutation into popular comedies with or without music "chanchada"[3] would become the most prolific and successful genre, and hundreds of such films were made by various companies from the mid-1930s until the late 1950s. Meanwhile, subtitled Hollywood products found no major obstacles to their hegemony. Literacy and other "cultural capital" differences among social groups worked also in Brazil to differentiate the markets for local films from the markets for imported ones, although many imported films also had a cross-class appeal.

WORLD WAR II AND BRAZILIAN FILM PRODUCTION

Although the constitution barred Vargas from succeeding himself in the 1938 elections, near the end of 1937 he cancelled the elections, dissolved the Congress, and assumed dictatorial powers under a new constitution. All political activity was prohibited.

[2] It is a clear sign of the relative underdevelopment of Brazilian film production vis-a-vis distribution and exhibition that by 1937 total investments in production were estimated at $1,200,000 while investments in distribution and exhibition reached about $50,000,000. Also in 1937, the annual revenue of American distributors in Brazil was approximately $3,000,000, of which 40% remained in Brazil to pay for operating expenses (Usabel, 1975, p. 356).

[3] Difficult to translate, this name has extremely disdainful connotations (inferior products for unsophisticated consumers, cultural trash). Based on comic actors made popular by radio and the live theatre, the chanchada genre had variants like the Carnaval film, and the satiric parody. These films' popularity decayed with the advent and diffusion of television.

The new regime, called *Estado Novo* (New State) was not only an authoritarian regime, but also one of the outstanding examples of Latin American populism.[4] The *Estado Novo* combined its authoritarian and repressive aspects with the struggle to attain a greater measure of economic independence, industrialization, and infrastructural modernization. Indicative planning and direct investment in basic industrial sectors were undertaken by the state. Labor was neutralized by means of paternalistic social legislation.

World War II brought further momentum to Brazilian industrialization. The advanced industrialized countries involved in the war could not pay for their purchases from developing countries with machinery and consumer goods, a situation which allowed Brazil (and other countries on the periphery of capitalism) to accumulate a relatively large reserve of foreign exchange. Vargas profited from the U.S.-Germany rivalry in order to secure financial and technical assistance from the U.S. for the construction of a large steel and iron plant deemed essential for the sustained progress of Brazilian industrialization.

This momentum towards state supported industrialization did not extend to local filmmaking. Although feature film production picked up in 1940, throughout the 1930s it suffered an overall decline, reaching a state of virtual paralysis in 1941 and 1942, when the usual distribution and exhibition bottlenecks coincided with war-related celluloid scarcity. As a comparison, in 1941 Argentina released 47 films, and 46 were produced in Mexico (Table 3).

Issued under Vargas' Estado Novo, a 1939 decree transferred the responsibility of establishing the proportion of Brazilian films to be shown to a newly created Department of Press and Propaganda. This decree also instituted the compulsory exhibition of at least one Brazilian feature for one week per year in every theatre. Santos Pereira (1973, p. 81) noted that "by 1939 several films attested to the degree of artistic and industrial maturity of Brazilian films, deserving a consideration less humiliating than a compulsory exhibition of seven days in the year".

In any case, the 1939 decree reinforced the policy of offering a modest screen quota to local production, but this quota was much lower than local production capability. Insofar as the U.S.-Brazil Commercial Treaty signed in 1935 forbade the imposition of foreign film import quotas, screen quotas were the main course of action open at the time, although screen quotas are only effective when set at higher levels than local filmmakers' production capability.

As in the cases of Argentina and Mexico, in Brazil the accelerated industrialization and urbanization processes brought about by government

[4] On populism see Boron (1981), Dos Santos (1974), and Laclau (1977).

policies designed to face the international economic depression and World War II, created an expanded audience for local film productions. A gradual growth in production occurred from 1943 until 1949, when 20 films were made.

The producing company Atlántida was the most important during these years. Founded in Rio de Janeiro in 1941 by a group of producers and technicians, Atlántida started an ambitious program. Initially, Atlántida was an attempt to produce films with localized content and atmosphere without necessarily falling into the conventions of the *chanchada*. Its first film was released in 1943, when there was renewed optimism in national industrialization and the war situation had interrupted the flow of European pictures, allowing more breathing space and screen time to local producers.

Associated with what at the time was the largest exhibition chain in the country, Atlántida began by making three or four films yearly, and had an important role in the gradual growth of local film production. Atlántida's association with an exhibition chain created a harmony between a fraction of Brazilian production and exhibition similar to the one extant from 1908 to 1911, a harmony based on vertical integration under the hegemony of national capital. In 1947, this exhibition chain became the company's principal stockholder. After that "the most apparent result of the confluence between the industrial and commercial interests [in local film] was the solidification of the *chanchada* and its proliferation for more than 15 years" resulting in its becoming the most lively genre in Brazilian filmmaking (Gonzaga and Salles Gomes, 1966, p. 88).

Atlántida produced about 85 films between 1943 and 1971. Working out of relatively modest studios, in its most important period (1945 to 1960) it produced a steady stream of inexpensive *chanchadas* and Carnaval films that were popular successes and filled the national film screen quota of the theatres affiliated with the owning circuit.[5]

On the political scene, as World War II progressed, domestic demands for the democratization of the authoritarian Estado Novo had grown stronger, forcing Vargas to promise general elections, scheduled to take place in December 1945. Although Vargas stated that he would not run for

[5] Paranagua (1981, p. 130) stated that the predominance and popular success of the *chanchada* has been considered humiliating by Brazilian intellectuals. Atlántida's success, based on the vertical integration of local capital, reinforced the belief of intellectuals and middle classes that serious films could only be made in Europe or the U.S. Recently, some Brazilian film critics have reevaluated the significance of the *chanchada*. Salles Gomes (1982) found in the genre elements of popular resistance to dominant imported cultural models. Bernardet analyzed the genre in terms of parody and aggression against such foreign models: "the aggression consists in reducing the [foreign] model to a level of underdevelopment. It produces a simultaneous devaluation both of the imposed model and of the originator of the parodic message" (quoted in Paranagua, 1981, p. 131).

the Presidency, his supporters began to stage a political campaign in his favor; meanwhile, Vargas gave a stronger populist tone to his economic policies so as to attract more popular support. An October, 1945, military coup frustrated Vargas' chances, and the elections gave the Presidency to Gral. Eurico Dutra (1945–1950).

The Dutra administration lifted import and foreign exchange controls, with the result that foreign exchange reserves accumulated during the war were used on imported (often luxury) consumer goods. Conservative interests regained a good part of the influence they had lost under Vargas, while the new economic climate stimulated a sharp increase in United States direct investment. It was within this general postwar atmosphere that the Vera Cruz experience took place.

THE CASE OF VERA CRUZ[6]

In a December 1945, decree the Dutra government increased the national film screen quota, establishing the compulsory exhibition in every theatre of at least three Brazilian feature films each year. Four years later (in 1949) a newly created Sindicato Nacional da Industria Cinematográfica (National Film Industry Union), organizing film producers interested in the further growth of Brazilian production, was instrumental in having the Congress pass a law allowing tax-free importation of studio and laboratory equipment.

These actions and an atmosphere of post war optimism led important industrial interests in São Paulo to initiate Brazilian film production on an industrial scale previously unknown in Brazil. This decision was made in the context of a general revitalization of Brazilian cinema and the founding of several new production companies. In São Paulo alone, more than 29 production companies were formed between 1949 and 1953. Most were unsuccessful, but Vera Cruz, followed by the considerably smaller Maristela and Multifilmes, placed Brazilian film production on a more ambitious plane.

The founding of the Vera Cruz production company in 1949 was an attempt by a powerful São Paulo industrial group to produce Brazilian films of international quality, able to compete both in the domestic and international markets. This project involved making larger numbers of high quality films. Galvao (1982) noted that this development must be seen in the context of a remarkable postwar growth in the city's cultural activities, a growth that accompanied the city's industrial development. São Paulo was the economic and industrial capital of Brazil.

[6] For more details concerning the circumstances surrounding Vera Cruz founding and its subsequent commercial failure, see Galvao (1982).

Matarazzo, an extremely successful industrialist, originated and supported an important modern theatre company in 1948. In 1949, his group founded the Vera Cruz company, and it was the main force behind the initiation of the São Paulo Museum of Modern Art and its prestigious Biennale in 1951.

The success of the theatre company encouraged the Matarazzo group, and it was expected that Vera Cruz would repeat that success, creating a Brazilian film production of international quality practically ex nihilo. The group that originated Vera Cruz abhorred the *chanchada* genre. Vera Cruz aimed to integrate Brazilian locales and themes with international technical and narrative standards ("international" meaning styles developed in advanced capitalist countries).

Vera Cruz benefited from the 1949 tax-free equipment importation law, and everything was done on a grand scale: massive and sophisticated studios were built, the most advanced equipment was imported, and distinguished European technicians were contracted. In short, the complexity and sophistication of the production system designed and implemented at the Vera Cruz studios surpassed all previous efforts in Brazilian cinematography. Very highly capitalized vis-a-vis other Brazilian production companies, Vera Cruz was equipped and organized on the basis of the Hollywood studio model, at a time when in Hollywood itself this model was undergoing stress and decline as a consequence of the changes brought about by competition with television. Alberto Cavalcanti, a Brazilian filmmaker who had gained international recognition by his participation in the French avant-garde and English documentary movements, was hired to direct the company.[7]

Even though the Matarazzo industrial group had been remarkably successful in other economic endeavors, their perception of economically viable filmmaking in Brazil would not lead to success for Vera Cruz. In the same fashion as the Brazilian filmmakers of the early 1930s, the Matarazzo circle aimed at quality production, without systematically taking into account distribution and exhibition structures. Paranagua (1981, p. 133) stated that Vera Cruz authorities had to face a permanent "dumping" of foreign (mostly American) films. An average of 500 films were imported each year, and were licensed to be exhibited for five years, which meant that an average of 2,500 foreign feature films were being shown commercially in any given year. In order to maintain a permanent lobbying position, the local branches of the large U.S. companies were represented by an organization called Brazilian Cinema Association, and the Motion Picture Export Association maintained a permanent representative in Brazil.

The Rio de Janeiro *chanchadas* were made at very low cost and had secured exhibition channels. Unlike Atlántida, the Rio de Janeiro company

[7] For Cavalcanti's conception of cinema see his book *Filme e Realidade,* 1977.

that was integrated into an extended exhibition circuit and produced films that were appreciated by the popular sectors that were the main audiences for local films, Vera Cruz aimed at the international market even before securing a foothold in its domestic market.

In its first steps, Vera Cruz geared its productions to compete in the international market, and Columbia Pictures was put in charge of the international distribution of Vera Cruz output. But Columbia Pictures was not very interested in the promotion of Brazilian films, and Vera Cruz did not have the resources to establish its own international distribution channels.[8]

Even though Vera Cruz' first films presented clear technical improvements, foreign markets proved practically inaccessible, while the local market was very slow in yielding returns commensurate with the company's high initial investments. The company's authorities had disregarded the fact that the Rio de Janeiro *chanchadas* were made at very low cost and had secure exhibition channels. Vera Cruz investments were too high compared to the profit potential of national films in the domestic market, of which they occupied only a small fraction.

Financially cornered, the company contracted short term loans at high interest rates, first from private banks and later from official banking institutions. Believing that more films would accelerate the rate of return and would give the company more bargaining power via-a-vis exhibitors, Vera Cruz turned to the domestic market and increased production so as to be able to rely on a large pool of films for distribution. Of course this bargaining power could never compete with that of foreign distributors or with the vertical integration of Atlántida.

Vera Cruz turned to the production of popular comedies, while continuing to turn out a more polished product. Although some of these low budget films were popular successes, the permanent high costs of the company's mode of organization (large and expensive studios, technical and artistic personnel under permanent contract) made these successes insufficient to make the company profitable.

In 1953 the company produced its greatest success: *O Cangaceiro,* inaugurating a whole new genre: the film about the adventures of bandits in the Brazilian northeastern region. This film was awarded prizes at the Cannes festival. In a 1968 survey of Brazilian film critics, *O Cangaceiro* was overwhelmingly voted the best Brazilian film ever made. The success of this film, however, came too late, and only Columbia Pictures profited from its international distribution.

Vera Cruz began to experience serious financial difficulties in 1953, and by 1954 it could only finish four films already in production thanks to

[8] Historically, in Latin America only the state has had the resources to organize foreign distribution of national films (see discussion of Pel-Mex in Mexico in Chapter 4 and Embrafilme, below).

an intense support campaign launched by the press and cultural circles. In 1954, the company was in the middle of its final crisis, and under the intervention of the São Paulo State Bank. Between its founding in 1949 and its bankruptcy in 1954 Vera Cruz finished 18 features and two shorts. A few years later, under the banner of Brazil Cinematográfica, the Vera Cruz studios were offered for lease to other producers.

When Vera Cruz went bankrupt the smaller São Paulo companies also collapsed. These failures had deep repercussions in Brazilian cinema. It was clearly perceived that an industrial structure for film production was not in itself sufficient to guarantee the development of Brazilian cinema. This perception was followed by renewed pressures on the provincial and federal government to obtain more adequate state protection, and by the formulation of new production alternatives encompassing an independent cinema. For the first time, an artisan mode of production was adopted by choice, not circumstance (Galvao, 1982, p. 278). A few years later, in the early 1960s, the first films of the *Cinema Novo* movement would be excellent examples of this new attitude towards film production.

State Protection: Renewed Demands

The years spanned by the Vera Cruz experience saw the continued efforts by economic, artistic, and technical groups interested in the growth of a viable Brazilian film industry to gain better state protection, and the beginning of these efforts also took place at a moment when the last Vargas government (1950-1954) was struggling to gain more space for national capitalists. As a matter of fact, it was the previous demise of Vargas authoritarian Estado Novo (in 1945) that opened the possibility for the mobilization of intellectuals and their renewed activity in Brazilian cultural life. Such democratization took place within a general ideological framework of nationalism, the search for a more autonomous way of Brazilian industrial development and, paradoxically enough, found expression in the last Vargas government (1950-1954), a government that attempted to maintain the development process under the relative hegemony of Brazilian capital. This political and cultural atmosphere, and the failure of the São Paulo production companies, sparked a renewed mobilization of Brazilian interests related to film production that led to a coherent articulation of state protection demands that would continue from then on. Also from that moment, every time that these interests attempted to gain better operating conditions for local filmmaking, they had to face the combined counterlobbying efforts of the MPEA's representative and Brazilian exhibitors dependent on foreign films (Santos Pereira, 1973, pp. 226-357, esp. p. 247).

Profiting from a wave of discontent with the economic and social policies of the Dutra government, and based on a broad coalition of workers, industrialists, and the urban middle class, Vargas regained the presidency in the 1950 election. But by the early 1950s the Vargas program of state-led industrialization, a program that various sectors of the ruling elites could consider appropriate to an international conjuncture marked by economic depression and world war, encountered renewed hostility from foreign and domestic conservative interests. Goulart, Vargas' Minister of Labor, angered conservatives and the military by proposing a doubling of the minimum wage. The Brazilian Congress, dominated by traditional rural forces, delayed and resisted Vargas' proposals for the creation or consolidation of state enterprises in basic economic activities, in the same fashion as it resisted the presidential proposal to create a National Film Institute to reorganize and extend the state protectionist structure for Brazilian cinema.

In 1950, Vargas formed a National Cinema Commission under the direction of Cavalcanti, charged with proposing a project to create a National Film Institute that would administer a far-ranging state protection scheme. Submitted to Congress, this project was never approved. The only door open to the Vargas government was to increase the screen quota for Brazilian films. A November 1951, decree established the quota at one local film for each set of eight foreign films exhibited, a measure that proved extremely difficult to enforce.

The renewed efforts of the forces favoring increased protection for local filmmaking found expression in the organization of two Congresses of the Brazilian Film Industry, the first in 1952 and the second a year later. The first of these meetings took place at a time when Congress was considering the Cavalcanti project to create a National Film Institute. The second took place in São Paulo in December 1953, and called attention to the serious problems experienced by the São Paulo studios, problems that shortly after would cause their demise. These conferences called for limits on foreign films through import quotas and taxation, and denounced the special treatment of foreign distributors who enjoyed favorable official exchange rates at which they were allowed to acquire dollars for remittance to their headquarters.

These and similar activities stirred public opinion and discussions in the Brazilian Congress and the press. The result of this agitation in favor of Brazilian film production was a series of laws and decrees in the 1950s and the 1960s. Most of these, however, were obtained from the governments that followed Vargas' death.

In the political arena, political lines of confrontation came into sharper focus when, in speeches to Congress, Vargas attacked foreign investors for compounding Brazil's balance of payment problems. When, in August 1954, the military informed Vargas that his choices were either to resign or be deposed, his chosen alternative was suicide.

Vargas' death marked the demise of the state-directed model (nationalist and populist in ideology) of more independent capitalist development over which he had presided since 1930. As in Argentina under Perón and in Chile under Ibañez (see Chapters 4 and 6) such a model, based on a compromise among the most relevant social forces, had reached its limits. In the case of Brazil, as in the other cases, two basic options were open— either a program of state-supported structural changes, or a modernized capitalist-dependent model based on the increased denationalization of Brazilian industry and the export of manufactured goods. While Vargas' political heirs favored the first course of action, their traditional enemies preferred the second. For a decade Brazil would be torn between these two alternatives.

THE INDECISIVE YEARS: 1954–1964

From Developmentalism to Radical Populism

Contrary to expectations, the failure of the large São Paulo companies did not result in a decline in production. Film production more than doubled during the 1950s, increasing from 20 in 1950 to 44 in 1958 (Table 3). This growth took place under the new banner of "developmentalism."

The 1955 presidential election put Kubitschek in office, with Goulart as Vice-President, and with the promise of achieving accelerated economic development. This economic growth, however, was to be sought within the framework of a "developmentalist" model that offered accelerated capitalist development as a solution to the problems of underdevelopment, an incremental growth based on massive foreign investment, to which Kubitschek offered generous advantages. A deeper denationalization of Brazilian industry followed after "national and international capital reached an agreement based on an economic development program that designated the sectors that could be penetrated by foreign capital" (Dos Santos, 1974, p. 448). Unprecedented short-term economic growth and further development of heavy industry were features of the Kubitschek years (1955–1960). The construction of Brasilia, the new capital, was considered one of the main symbols of the "developmentalist" outlook.

In the area of film, the new economic dynamism resulted in a stabilization of film production, improved working conditions for film technicians and other professionals, and renewed pressure towards legislation favoring local production. In 1956, Kubitschek created a Federal Film

Commission, an organization that enjoyed only consultative status, and whose recommendations were, overall, not implemented. This Commission was replaced in 1958 by GEIC (National Film Industry Study Group). Following GEIC recommendations, a December 1959 decree modified the previous Vargas screen quota, establishing a new one of 42 days per year for national films.

These years also saw the creation of State Commissions for Film in São Paulo and Guanabara, and the institution of a per-ticket bonus established by the city of São Paulo to supplement the box office intake of Brazilian films produced and exhibited in the city. At the same time, Brazilian films incorporating a more realistic view of Brazil were released, films that were different both from the old style *chanchada* and from the Vera Cruz Europeanized products. Although these films were relatively few in numbers, they prefigured the subsequent *Cinema Novo* movement.

The 1960 presidential elections saw the triumph of Quadros, former governor of São Paulo, accompanied by Goulart as Vice-President. Quadros campaigned on promises to end government corruption, and for a more independent foreign policy. Facing obstructionism from a conservative-dominated Congress, Quadros resigned after only seven months in office, expecting that a popular mobilization would bring him back to the presidency with wider powers. Popular sentiment, however, went in the direction of a constituional solution; Vice-President Goulart would become President.

Although Goulart was a wealthy rancher, and a populist politician in the tradition of Vargas, the right-wing military considered him a radical, and only accepted Goulart as President after a constitutional amendment instituted a parliamentary system of government in lieu of the previous presidential system. During Goulart's presidency (1961-1964) the confrontation between the alternative courses of action mentioned above (deeper socio-economic structural reforms, or a streamlined model of dependent development) came into sharper focus.

Paralyzed by the parliamentary system, Goulart's administration produced very few changes at first, but after a 1962 plebiscite that restored its former powers to the Presidency, Goulart drafted a program that included agrarian reform and other economic and political changes. Goulart's victory, however, had not changed the fact that most members of Congress were against his reform proposals. A growing polarization swept the country, with popular mobilizations in favor of deeper reforms on the one hand, and a growing apprehension among the conservative forces—the large landowners, the bourgeoisie upper echelons, the military, and the representatives of foreign investment—on the other. In the midst of this growing polarization, Goulart was overthrown by a military coup that was supported not only by the above groups but also by the industrial bourgeoisie, and sectors of the middle classes. This military coup enjoyed wholesale U.S. support.

During Goulart's government, GEIC, converted now to an Executive Study Group with wider powers (GEICINE), continued its work towards better conditions for local filmmaking. Following one of its multiple recommendations, the national film screen quota was raised in 1963 from 42 to 56 days per year. The creation of a National Film Institute was once more recommended and once more postponed.

The Goulart years also saw the consolidation of the *Cinema Novo* movement, a protean denomination that incorporated a wide variety of styles, themes, and forms (shorts, documentaries, features). During the Goulart government the Marxist and nationalist left expected that a peoples' mobilization would force the government to implement measures of radical social change. *Cinema Novo* was born in this context of the radicalization of intellectuals and their attempts to reach the popular sectors with literacy campaigns and culture for the people. *Cinema Novo* filmmakers searched for new approaches to Brazilian reality, specifically to the realities of underdevelopment, poverty, marginality, and exploitation that as a rule had not appeared in Brazilian films before. In their attempt to make independent films (independent both in terms of critical content and non-industrial modes of production), *Cinema Novo* filmmakers drew inspiration from the theory and practice of Italian neo-realism and the production strategies of the French *nouvelle vague* (low-budget *auteur* films).[9]

The movement attained international stature when five of the twenty-seven films produced in 1962 won prizes at festivals, resulting in international distribution. But despite individual successes, *Cinema Novo* films were seen mostly by audiences of students and intellectuals, and had difficulty in reaching wider audiences, used either to the Hollywood products or the local *chanchada*. The 1964 military coup created a new and difficult situation for critical Brazilian filmmakers, and their situation became even more difficult when increased government repression began in 1968. The following section offers an overview of the 1964-1982 evolution of the military governments as a background for state policies towards local cinema in the same period.

MILITARY GOVERNMENTS 1964-1982: FROM REPRESSION TO *ABERTURA*

The new military government severely limited all forms of popular participation in political life, giving itself all the powers it felt necessary through

---

[9] For an excellent introduction to the *Cinema Novo* movement, see Johnson and Stam, 1982, pp. 30-51; see also Paranagua, 1981, pp. 141-153.

the proclamation of Institutional Acts. Politicians were deprived of their political rights, student unions dispersed, labor unions tightly controlled, and peasant leagues outlawed. The "bureaucratic-authoritarian"[10] regime in Brazil followed an overall course of encouraging a deeper penetration of foreign capital, repression of labor and most forms of political opposition, and suppression of dissent in cultural life. Such repression and censorship were especially harsh in the 1968–1972 period.

A context of high unemployment, lower wages, and increasing participation of foreign companies in the Brazilian economy brewed widespread dissatisfaction with the military regime. This dissatisfaction found expression in the 1965 elections for state governors, and in popular music, films, and the legitimate stage.

Dissatisfaction and protests increased by 1967, when Marshal Costa e Silva succeeded General Castelo Branco as president. Costa e Silva began by allowing a somewhat wider range of political activity. Facing increasing protests and some signs of independence from the still-functioning Congress and the judiciary, the extreme right-wing military groups produced a coup-within-a-coup and pressured Costa e Silva to promulgate an extremely repressive Fifth Institutional Act that, among other provisions, gave the President dictatorial powers, suspended the constitution, closed down the Congress, and discontinued writs of habeas corpus.

Due to an incapacitating illness, Costa e Silva was replaced in 1969 by General Garrastazú Médici (1969–1974) who presided over years of both unprecedented economic growth and a conspicuous presence of the state repressive apparatus. One of the distinctive traits of the Brazilian variety of bureaucratic-authoritarianism was that not all features of democratic regimes were abolished. Elections featuring government controlled political parties continued, and a 1972 election made clear that the vast majority of Brazilians were against censorship and repression.

In military summit meetings, General Geisel was selected to succeed Medici. Geisel took office in March 1974, and promised a policy of *distensão,* a gradual reduction in inflexible rule and the beginnings of a transi-

---

[10] In bureaucratic authoritarian regimes the popular sectors are excluded from all forms of participation in political and social decision making; the main actors in the power coalition are high-level technocrats (military and civilian) closely associated with foreign capital. This new elite either eliminates or severly conditions electoral competition and imposes tight controls on popular political participation. Public policy's main concern is the promotion of advanced industralization in terms very favorable to multinational capital. Examples of this type of state or political regime are Brazil after the 1964 coup, Argentina 1966–1970 and after 1976, Chile after the 1973 coup, and the military regime in Uruguay. (see O'Donnell, 1973; Collier, 1979). Concerning the type of industrialization promoted in Brazil, Burns stated: "While industrialization grew rapidly under the military, it embodied many weaknesses: a concentration on goods for the wealthy and middle class, a dependency on foreign investment, technology, and markets, a denationalization of Brazilian-owned industry, a low rate of labor absorption since it was capital intensive, ecological threats and pollution, and regressive income redistribution" (1980, p. 531).

tion toward a civilian constitutional regime. Geisel decreased censorship and checked the state repressive apparatus. This policy of *distensão* was the basis for the government's willingness to listen to Brazilian producers' and filmmakers' demands, and for important changes in state policy toward local cinema, that opened the door to a new and redirected vitality in Brazilian filmmaking.

There might have been an attempt to present an image of a more enlightened authoritarianism taking concrete steps in the cultural arena, of which cinema had high national and international visibility. There may also have been an attempt to present a cultural image different from the *chanchada,* and *Cinema Novo* directors were the only directors who could do it.

The Geisel government had to face increasing economic problems, workers' strikes and student mobilizations, while important sectors of the bourgeoisie began to voice opposition. The increasingly vocal opposition and a relaxation in political repression were apparent when in 1978 an opposition front gathered 44% of the votes in the electoral college to elect the next president.

In March 1979, the official candidate, General Figueiredo, assumed the presidency for a six-year term, and announced the intention to preside over a continued transition to democratic rule. *Distensão* gave way to *abertura,* a gradual opening of the political system that was immediately translated into action with a comprehensive political amnesty. The sharp decrease in repression and censorship, and freer play of political forces, however, has not extended to labor rights or to any challenge to the basic model of bureaucratic-authoritarian rule (Rabben, 1982). While a wider incorporation of elite sectors as a legitimation procedure has effectively taken place, the future evolution of such a political regime is still an open question.

State Policies and Brazilian Filmmaking, 1964–1982

As noted above, from 1964 to 1968 the young *Cinema Novo* filmmakers were part of a broad cultural movement that opposed the military government, a cultural movement that also found expression in the legitimate stage and in popular music. Although *Cinema Novo* did not decline, its practice could not escape the general crisis of leftist intellectuals, becoming somewhat more pessimistic and increasingly metaphorical in films' references to current events. This trend became even more apparent after the 1968 coup-within-a-coup caused a sharp increase in repression and censorship.

The government attitude toward a local cinema during the 1968–1972 years was a complex one. While new state organizations (National Film Institute, created in 1966; Embrafilme, created in 1969) supported the expansion of local film production, censorship made work impossible for some *Cinema Novo* directors, who chose instead to emigrate. Glauber Rocha, Rui Guerra, and Carlos Diegues left Brazil, as well as many other well known figures in the theatre and in popular music. Consequently, while film production tripled from 30 features in 1961 to 94 in 1971 (Table 3), some of the original *Cinema Novo* directors did not have a predominant role.

Under these conditions of increased censorship, the late 1960s and early 1970s also saw the growth of a São Paulo-centered underground film movement, an extreme form of independent production made under the most repressive phase of the Brazilian bureaucratic-authoritarian regime. Censorship and exhibitors' lack of interest left only film societies and universities as exhibition sites for the underground productions.

Beginning in the early 1970s, an increased national films screen quota and the success of some comedies with erotic overtones originated the *pornochanchada*, a form of pseudo-erotic comedy (Paranagua, 1981, p. 156) produced in many cases by exhibitors. Through this genre, these exhibitors turned producers are able to compete with television, offering something that cannot be shown on the small screen, and they also benefit from the Brazilian film quota.[11]

The most remarkable achievements of the military regime in the area of state film policy were the creation of the National Film Institute in 1966, and Embrafilme in 1969.[12] These institutions have to be seen in the context of a complex process of supression-cooptation of political and cultural dissent, and a style of state participation in the country's cultural production that paralleled the state intervention in the economy (Ianni, 1978; for the style of state intervention in the economy see Evans, 1979).

The state intervened to support national production, but without directly confronting the importation of foreign films. As in other areas of the economy, the state project was to support national film production until it could compete better with the foreign products introduced in the Brazilian market, thus maintaining the equilibrium of the three basic sectors of the economy: national, foreign, and state capital (Andrade, 1980; Evans, 1979).

[11] Historically, whenever and wherever exhibitors were forced to exhibit a large number of national films, they attempted to produce their own, in many cases as inexpensively as possible. When this happened in England, such films were called "quota quickies" (see Montagu, 1968, Ch. 7).

[12] For a detailed presentation on both the National Film Institute and Embrafilme, see Johnson, 1982 a, b.

The National Film Institute was created in 1966 on the basis of the prexistent GEICINE project, itself the heir to all previous attempts to create such an institution since the commission organized by the Vargas government in 1950. The Institute was given relatively wide powers as a regulatory agency of the Brazilian film industry. One of the most important aspects of its activity was the administration of a subsidy in which all Brazilian films participated according to their box office success. A small number of films considered culturally outstanding received an additional subsidy. The Institute also established a program of film production financing, and introduced a series of measures designed to curb exhibitors' underreporting of box office revenues, a practice that was particularly damaging to national producers. The subsidy program has been an important source of support for local filmmakers, and has continued under Embrafilme.

Embrafilme was created in 1969, formally as a mixed ownership enterprise, but it had in reality only nominal private capital participation. It was subordinated to the Ministry of Education and Culture. Although originally created only to promote and distribute Brazilian films abroad, throughout the 1970s the enterprise increased the scope of its activities substantially, incorporating and expanding the National Film Institute functions.

The *distensão* policy noted above, the first sign of which appeared in 1972, made possible a 1972 Congress of the Brazilian Film Industry organized by the National Film Institute, where the various sectors could express their points of view. A group of film producers presented a Brazilian Cinema Project that read in part: "Our films fill only 23 percent of exhibition time, while the rest is filled by foreign productions that are imported without restrictions and lightly taxed. In this context, national cinema cannot expand as would be required by its functions of enhancing the information and social integration of our people, and diffussing our artistic, historical, and cultural heritage" (quoted in Santos Pereira, 1973, p. 100). Brazilian producers suggested that the National Film Institute be transformed into a National Film Council, authorized to establish annual quotas for the importation of foreign films according to the interests of the development of a national film industry. Embrafilme was reorganized following most of the guidelines of the producers' project, with the important exception that it was not authorized to impose foreign films quotas, stressing supportive protectionism instead. With its powers expanded, Embrafilme was authorized to enter not only film distribution but also production and exhibition.

In 1973, Embrafilme began to act as a domestic distributor and has in time become the second largest in the country; the first being Cinema International Corporation which in Brazil is in charge of distributing the films handled by MGM, Paramount, Walt Disney, and Universal. Embrafilme has also seen a remarkable growth in foreign distribution, its original area of activity, opening offices in France and the U.S., and steadily expanding into the Latin American market. As a film distribution agency the enterprise follows strictly commercial guidelines.

Embrafilme became a decisive force in domestic film production beginning in 1974, when President Geisel named *Cinema Novo* filmmaker Roberto Farias as director, an appointment that was an unequivocal part of the *"distensão"* policy.[13] It was the Farias directorship (1974–1979) that gave new momentum to distribution, and to a program of coproductions with independent producers. In 1975, Embrafilme was reorganized and expanded, incorporating the executive functions of the National Film Institute, while the legislative functions relative to film were entrusted to CONCINE, a National Cinema Council. The members of this Council are representatives of various government ministries, and of commercial, professional and artistic sectors involved in national cinema.

While Embrafilme has continued to administer the preexistent subsidy program, it also provides financial assistance to Brazilian filmmakers through low interest loans (operating as a film bank), coproduction, and advances on distribution. Between 1973 and 1979, Embrafilme signed coproduction contracts with 89 different companies for the production of 114 feature films plus 19 pilots for television series (Johnson, 1982b).

Embrafilme's decision to grant financial support to a production is made on the basis of a point system in which producers' and directors' previous records (including national and international festival prizes) are heavily weighted. It is this system that has enabled *Cinema Novo* directors to benefit from the enterprise organization. Many *Cinema Novo* filmmakers disavowed their previous rejection of industry and market requirements, thus opening the door to a new relationship with the state. Johnson (1982a, p. 3) stated "there has been a convergence of interests and a marriage of convenience between independent producers and Embrafilme."

All of the *Cinema Novo* directors returned to Brazil after 1972, and have been able to work with Embrafilme support, as part of the change in the military government policy. Decision to furnish financial assistance is made upon presentation of the script, without any further intervention by Embrafilme, a policy that has helped finance some films very critical of the repressive aspects or the social consequences of the Brazilian bureau-

---

[13] Embrafilme gained momentum under the Geisel government when feature films might have been seen as a mass medium allowing the government to test the social and cultural effects of *"distensão"* in mass communications before it was extended to wider diffusion mass media like television.

cratic-authoritarian regime and its economic policies.[14] The enterprise does not act as a censorship agency; actually, some of the films that received Embrafilme support have been banned by censorship, which is delegated to a different branch of the state apparatus.[15]

Brazilian film production is not concentrated in large studios; Embrafilme has not sought either to repeat the Vera Cruz experience, or to emulate the role of the state in Mexico. Film production in Brazil has remained relatively dispersed, undertaken by many small production companies, often headed by a film director. These companies usually average one film per year or less. This system creates a highly dispersed mode of production. In 1977, for instance, 65 different production companies produced 73 films, of which 24 were coproduced by Embrafilme. Although the enterprise has not attempted to concentrate production in large studios, some observers feel that the credit policy tends to favor a few large producers, and the number of films coproduced has indeed declined.

According to Andrade (1980) the Embrafilme policy has concentrated production in a few producers, so that "the independent production under the control of the director disappears, and the independent project of a cinema capable of affirming the value of Brazilian culture is lost." Embrafilme had some form of financial participation in the production of 75 films in 1975, 60 in 1976, 38 in 1977, and about 30 films in 1981, of which 15 were coproduced.

In the area of exhibition, Embrafilme has developed a program to acquire or lease theatres that are experiencing financial problems. Acting then as coproducer, distributor, and exhibitor, Embrafilme has created a peculiar form of vertical integration under the hegemony of the state, although exhibition is still its weakest link.

As in the case of state-led vertical integration in Mexico, the fact that Embrafilme operates both as producer or coproducer (with at least some cultural interests to attend to) and as a commercial distributor has caused some tension insofar as projects funded and considered culturally relevant by one branch of the enterprise are sometimes seen as of insufficient commercial potential by the same enterprise's distribution agency, that tends

---

[14] Films' ideological effects can be seen as a complex result of their mode of production, distribution, and consumption, overdetermined by a complex context of economic, political, and cultural-ideological conjunctural variables. This means that critical films in terms of content need not have a strongly oppositional effect when shown under normal commercial circumstances (that allow neither space nor time for subsequent collective discussion) and reaching mostly a middle class audience. Since the wide diffusion of color television, film goers in Brazil belong mostly to the urban middle and upper classes, and 50% of the film market is concentrated in Rio de Janeiro and São Paulo.

[15] Although it cannot be presented in any detail here, Althusser's distinction between repressive and ideological state apparatuses (1971) and their relative autonomy appears highly relevant to the comprehension of this and other similar processes.

to relegate such films. As in Mexico[16] the partial vertical integration under the hegemony of the state does not guarantee perfect harmony among the various branches of the enterprise, not to mention the lack of harmony between Embrafilme as producer and government censorship as an arm of the state repressive apparatus in the area of mass communication. The state has maintained a fluctuating combination of a repressive relationship with Brazilian cinema through censorship, and a supportive role for local filmmaking through state protection.

Expectedly, Embrafilme action has been surrounded by controversy, and while some critics feel that the enterprise favored an elitist form of cultural film with relative disregard for market conditions, others state that there has been a relative neglect of cultural functions and too much concentration on the commercial aspects of filmmaking. Others see in the enterprise's organization and modus operandi a guarantee of stylistic and thematic diversity and a source of sustained support for Brazilian cinema.

It should not be forgotten that the organization is also involved in a wide array of cultural activities (cooperation with "cinematecas," publication of books and the magazine Filme Cultura, production of documentaries, etc), although some critical observers claim that most educational aspects of Embrafilme have been relatively neglected in favor of its activity in commercial film production and distribution.[17]

Although Embrafilme added the all important supportive elements of state coproduction and distribution, historically the most consistent basis of state protection for the local film industry in Brazil has been and continues to be the screen quota. No import quota has been implemented, but the importation of foreign films has been limited through a number of measures that have made such importation more expensive. Although the local producers' Brazilian Cinema Project, that recommended the formation of the Cinema Council and the restructuring of Embrafilme, also recommended the imposition of foreign film quotas, this last recommendation was not adopted. Brazil is a signatory of a number of international commercial treaties (of which the U.S.-Brazil 1935 treaty is a precedent) that guarantee the free international circulation of films. The screen quota itself has reduced the space for foreign films, and measures like the compulsory use of Brazilian laboratories to make copies (implemented in 1973) and higher censorship fees (beginning in 1977) have made the commercial-

[16] In Mexico "the state as theatre-owner sabotages the state as film producer in favor of private producers. Films produced by the state in 1977 and 1978 have still not been shown ...while privately produced films are shown a few months after they are finished, especially if they belong to Televicine, which in all probability will become the film monopoly as it now is in television" (Perez Turrent and Turner, 1980).

[17] For instance, it is claimed that no film school has been organized, and there is no protection for 16mm films or other "little media" of wider potential difussion (Paranagua, 1981, p. 165).

ization of foreign films in Brazil more expensive. These can be seen as indirect protectionist measures.

The national film screen quota stands now at 140 days per year (since 1979, see Table 9), and as a result of the state's expanded intervention in all aspects of film-related activities, from 1974 to 1978 the number of spectators for Brazilian films went from 30 to 60 million, while the total income for Brazilian films went from 13 to 38 million dollars. Brazilian cinema doubled its audience and almost tripled its revenue during these years (Andrade, 1980).

All attempts to increase the national film quota met stiff resistance from exhibitors and the local representatives of U.S.-based companies. The military governments began by ratifying, in 1967, the extant 56 days per year screen quota until a new criterion could be determined.[18] A new criterion was established by resolution N.38, in 1970, amidst heated controversy between local producers and exhibitors, including press conferences, press releases, etc. The new resolution established a screen quota of 112 days per year. For all practical purposes the screen quota for local films was doubled.

Brazilian exhibitors reacted very strongly against the new quota, initiating presentations of their point of view to the President and the Minister of Education. Exhibitors maintained that the new screen quota meant bankruptcy for them. Producers, on the other hand, made public their support for the National Film Institute. The pressures of exhibitors were successful and in January 14, 1971, the quota was reduced from 112 to 98 days per year. This reduction was not considered adequate by the exhibitors, who continued applying pressure on the government, obtaining the resignation of the Institute's director, and a further reduction of the screen quota to 84 days per year. After Embrafilme's reorganization, in 1975, the national film quota was again brought to the level of 112 days per year, and since then it has been increased to 140 days per year (Table 9).

The increased screen quota and higher importation costs have further reduced the space for foreign films, forcing foreign distributors to import fewer films and to be more selective. Screen quotas, however, have not eliminated the laws of the market within each market preserve, and there is stiff competition among Brazilian films within the space opened to them by the compulsory screen quota.

---

[18] By the end of 1969, and due to the large number of local films finished and without exhibition prospects, the Film Institute ordered an additional 7 days of compulsory exhibition. This additional screen quota was ordered while waiting for the results of a commission formed by film producers, exhibitors, and functionaries of the Institute, created to analyze the protectionist system. The film backlog lends support to the contention that the extant film quota underestimated the capability for local film production.

The MPEA and Brazilian exhibitors resisted the protectionist legislation and have initiated legal procedures to contest it in court. At the same
time, in 1978 a MPEA representative promised to lobby the U.S. Congress
to allow freer importation of Brazilian products into the U.S. (of which
shoes were an important component) if Brazil did not impose restrictions
to the free flow of U.S. films and the remittance of profits (Andrade, 1980).

Two years earlier, in 1976, Jack Valenti, head of the MPEA, met in
Jamaica with the Brazilian Minister of Finance, and arranged for U.S. distributors to be excluded from a decree that limited to one-third the proportion of profits that all foreign companies could remit abroad. Valenti
promised in exchange to lobby in the U.S. Congress for better terms for
the importation of Brazilian products into the U.S. The effect of the Brazilian decree "would have cost us several million dollars per year, with the
possibility of sterner measures later, Valenti told MPEA client companies"
(*Variety*, May 19, 1976, p. 1; 126).

There has also been a long struggle between filmmakers and Embrafilme on one side, and exhibitors and U.S. distributors on the other, regard-
ing shorts. A 1977 measure made mandatory the exhibition of a Brazilian
short with each foreign film shown. Once more Jack Valenti, head of the
MPEA, went to Brazil to lobby against the measure. The combined lobbying of MPEA and theatre owners succeeded in delaying for three years the
implementation of the measure. Finally implemented in 1980, exhibitors
began to produce their own hastily produced shorts so as to receive the
percentage of the gross payable to short producers. In this way, the intention to utilize shorts as vehicles of cultural innovation and as a training
ground for new directors and technicians was sidetracked (Paranagua,
1981, p. 165).

Increased state protection in Brazil has had a number of effects. It
has already been mentioned that it has led to increased production (Table
3) and to more revenues for Brazilian producers. Increased protectionism
has also led some of the U.S.-based companies operating in Brazil to produce films that benefit from the protectionist provisions. Cinema International Corporation, for instance, not only distributes U.S. films and owns
some theatres in Brazil, but has also entered production, finding ways to
comply with the legal definition of "Brazilian films" so as to enjoy state
protection (Bernardet, 1979, Ch. 1).[19]

The proliferation of *pornochanchada* films can also be seen as an
unintended effect of increased protectionism coupled with censorship
traditionally hard on oppositional ideologies but now soft on increasingly

[19] Guback (1969) pointed out the remarkable extent of a similar phenomenon in Western
Europe throughout the 1960s.

explicit sexual themes. Beginning in the early 1970s, an increased national films screen quota and the success of some comedies with erotic overtones originated the *pornochanchada,* a form that would become one of the most prolific and distinctive Brazilian genres throughout the 1970s and early 1980s (see p. 67). Exhibitors produce *pornochanchada* films as a way to make up for the losses of revenue caused by the exhibition of fewer foreign films and by television inroads into sizeable sectors of the audience.

Embrafilme's action in supporting a number of quality films can also be seen as representing the cultural interests of the state and its attempt not to disassociate completely from the cultural interests of intellectual sectors of society. The country's image in foreign countries might have also been a factor, as Embrafilme entered production and distribution in the early 1970s when the combination of a higher screen quota and ideological censorship seemed to leave *pornochanchada* as the only viable genre.[20]

Despite the remarkable growth in feature film production, relatively few Brazilian films are shown on television, where the film quotas do not apply. Even though Brazilian films have taken over part of the large screens, the television small screen is still a preserve of foreign production. In 1973, Rio de Janeiro television stations showed 1446 features, of which only 10 were Brazilian. In 1974, of 1704 films shown only 34 were Brazilian. In 1975 among 1,329 films, 6 were Brazilian.

As noted above, the market for Brazilian films has grown as a consequence of Embrafilme's action. From 1974 to 1978, domestic spectators for Brazilian films doubled (from 30 to 61 million), while spectators for foreign films went from 170 to 149 million. Following a worldwide trend, however, the number of theatres diminished, and decreased from around 3,000 theatres in 1969 to 2,318 in 1979.[21] The great majority of Brazilian theatres are privately owned, and Embrafilme owns or leases only a few theatres. As an exhibition alternative for independent filmmakers, in 1979 a group of film directors organized an exhibition cooperative that allowed them wider participation in decision-making than is possible in a bureaucratic organization like Embrafilme. Early in 1981, however, Embrafilme took over the administration of several of the cooperative's theatres, as the cooperative was experiencing severe financial difficulties.

With increased film production, reduced theatre outlets, and very few sales to local television, it is not surprising that Embrafilme has renewed its efforts to reach foreign markets. By 1981, 58% of its foreign

[20] According to Johnson (1982a, p. 24) "most of the films that would be considered "quality" products are linked to Embrafilme in some way, either through financing, coproduction, or distribution."

[21] This figure, quoted by Paranagua (1981) is much lower than the Unesco figure in Table 1.

revenue originated in other Latin American countries, while the rest came mostly from Eastern and Western European television (*Variety*, March 25, 1981, p. 75; 92).

Both Brazilian television and Embrafilme are very much interested in foreign markets. In 1977, Embrafilme organized, in Brasilia, the first International Congress for the Commercialization of Films in Spanish and Portuguese. Brazil proposed the creation of a Common Market for Films, with screen quotas to be shared by the market member countries (Farias, 1982). The Brazilian proposal suggested that each participating country reserve 30% of its domestic market for national films, and an additional 20% for films of the other Spanish- and Portuguese-speaking nations, thus leaving 50% of each market for international (mostly U.S.) distributors. The countries included in the proposal were Argentina, Colombia, Mexico, Spain, Paraguay, Peru, Portugal, Uruguay, and Venezuela. Paranagua (1981, p. 167) notes that this proposal, not yet implemented, is very favorable to Brazil, which is now the most important film producer in Latin America. The MPEA, however, is bound to oppose this proposal, as its control of distribution in other Latin America countries is much greater than the 50% allowed in the Brazilian plan. Meanwhile, Brazil has already signed bilateral agreements with Argentina and Portugal.

The momentum of state intervention and support for local filmmaking came under the Geisel government (1974-1979). The new government (Gen. Figueiredo) replaced *Cinema Novo* director Farias by a career diplomat who stated that his administration would be more technocratic and stress rentability (Amorim, quoted in Paranagua, 1981). The new administration has reduced state investments in film.

CONCLUDING REMARKS

This presentation of the Brazilian experience in filmmaking and state protection has stressed the essential role of state protection for the growth of national film production in developing countries, as well as the various forms that such support can take, and the fluctuations suffered by protectionist policies according to overall political circumstances. The presentation has also attempted not to gloss over some of the several ambiguities and dilemmas that such intervention entails.

One of the particularities in the development of Brazilian film production has been that the country's distinctive Luso-American linguistic and cultural heritage acted as a protective barrier against the introduction of Argentine and Mexican films for the popular sector of cinema goers. On the other hand, their Portuguese language precluded Brazilian films from gaining any significant position among popular sectors in the rest of Latin America. Only recently some of the quality Brazilian films made with Embrafilme support have gained an audience among students, intellectuals, and middle classes in other Latin American countries, where these films are exhibited with Spanish subtitles.

The following chapters focus on countries with smaller domestic markets, where for a variety of reasons the role of the state is even more crucial.

Chapter 6
Film Production in Chile, 1930–1980

The attempts to organize a film industry in Chile after the advent of sound are a clear example of the problems faced by such an endeavor in a capitalist-dependent country with an intermediate-sized market. In these cases, and barring very strong and consistent protectionist policies, U.S.-based multinationals and national distributors handling European productions supply most of the films, while the fractions of the market that cannot read subtitles or prefer films spoken in Spanish are supplied by Argentine, Mexican, and some Spanish productions. For countries like Chile, Colombia, Peru, Venezuela (and Cuba before 1959), the possibilities of attaining continuity of film production on an industrial basis were even slimmer than in Argentina, Brazil, or Mexico.[1]

EARLY ATTEMPTS

The 1929 economic crisis deeply unsettled Chile's economic patterns. The value of exports declined from $277.4 million in 1929 to $34.1 million in 1932, resulting in a drastic reduction in the country's capacity to import and bringing about the substitution of export-oriented mining for domestic market-oriented manufacturing as the dynamic sector of the economy.

[1] Unless otherwise noted, the basic references for this chapter are Keen and Wasserman (1980), Cavarozzi and Petras (1974), Ossa Coo (1971), Godoy Quezada (1966), and Chanan (1976).

By July 1931, widespread discontent and a massive general strike caused President Ibañez del Campo to resign and go into exile. The new Chilean government reacted to the drastic reduction in exports by imposing strict controls on all foreign exchange operations. Exchange transactions were geared to the importation of prime necessities, and the quantity and quality of foreign films released in Chile decreased accordingly. Affiliates of the large U.S. distribution companies, however, found means to secure their revenues in dollars and to channel them to New York via Argentina. Some U.S. distributors reinvested part of their blocked funds in Chilean enterprises to reduce losses from currency depreciation. United Artists ceased operating in Chile in August 1932, and did not reopen its office there until the end of 1936 (Usabel, 1975, pp. 377–80).

After several months of political instability, a caretaker regime installed in September 1932, organized new elections and a return to civilian rule. Arturo Alessandri became president, supported by a coalition of political parties with right-of-center leanings, and presided over a process of partial economic recovery. Alessandri's policies eliminated the worst aspects of unemployment, but workers' wages and living conditions did not keep up with inflation; workers' protests were met with repression. U.S.-based interests continued controlling the mining sector, and large estates remained the dominant force in Chilean agriculture.

These conditions did not create a favorable investment climate for risky ventures, and only one feature film was made in Chile between 1930 and 1939. *Norte y Sur* was the first Chilean "talkie." It was directed by Jorge Delano, who in 1930 had gone to Hollywood to learn the new techniques. Technical equipment could not be imported, and Delano had to build an optical printer with the aid of technicians of the local branch of RCA. Released in 1934, this film included generous doses of folkloric music and dance, thus confirming the direction that a considerable segment of Latin American films would take in order to compete with foreign films. Although this film was both a critical and a box-office success, the production of local films became very difficult, and no other feature films were made until 1939 (Table 3). American and European films continued to provide the movie fare for the middle and upper classes, while the sectors of the audience partial to films spoken in Spanish were progressively taken over by the products of Argentina and Mexico that exhibited technical standards somewhat superior to what could be done in Chile at the time (Godoy Quezada, 1966, p. 105).

THE POPULAR FRONT GOVERNMENTS

Film production in Chile gained new momentum with the advent of the Popular Front government in 1938. The mobilization of workers, peasants, and the urban middle sectors facilitated a new political alliance: the Popular Front, an alliance of the Socialist, Communist, and Radical parties. Radical politician Aguirre Cerda was the alliance presidential candidate in 1938. He campaigned on an electoral platform of civil liberties and social reform, and was instrumental in the organization of CORFO (Production Development Corporation), a state institution devoted to the promotion of Chile's industrialization and infrastructural modernization. Import substitution industrialization was reinforced by the interruption in imports caused by World War II and by the various support policies implemented by the government. The number of workers rose accordingly, and the industrialization process was accompanied by an increase in workers' purchasing power that lasted until the end of the war and enlarged the potential public for local film productions. Four major factors determined the nature of Chilean industrialization:

a. A radical reduction in foreign exchange generated by exports, and a scarcity of imports during World War II.
b. Important government support measures, that in some cases prodded industrialists to act.
c. The planning role exercised by CORFO technicians.
d. U.S. economic support and technical assistance. The loans received by CORFO from U.S. public and private banks were always tied to the purchase of American goods and equipment (Cavarozzi and Petras, 1974, p. 512).

Five films were made in 1939, encouraged by the interruption in the flow of European films and the new economic and political conditions. All of these films concentrated on light and sentimental comedy, the dramatic *feuilleton,* and *folklorism* a superficial and idyllic view of the Latin American countryside that should be carefully distinguished from folklore. At this time, CORFO began to consider supporting the expansion of local film production.

In its 1939 general report, CORFO estimated that film production had the potential of becoming an important industrial activity in Chile, supported by a local and foreign market. CORFO's 1940 report was more cautious, acknowledging that the experience of other countries, especially Argentina, indicated that important funds and technical resources were necessary to give momentum to local film production. In December 1941, CORFO created Chile Films, a company designed to build and operate film production studios. The founding of Chile Films was an attempt to put Chilean film production on firmer ground.

Four films, including comedy, popular songs, and some light social criticism were made in 1941, and five were completed in 1942. Film production grew to seven in 1947, still under the momentum of the war and post-war economic impulse (Table 3). Competition for the sector of the audience that preferred films spoken in Spanish, however, was pronounced. The growth problems faced by the national film industries in Mexico, Argentina, and Brazil were replicated at a different level in smaller countries. In Chile, the massive presence of U.S.-based distributors took over most of the middle-sector audiences, while the sector of the audience preferring Spanish-speaking films found a steady supply of films made in Argentina and Mexico (especially in Mexico from 1942 on). Chilean filmmakers' difficulties were thus compounded. Godoy Quezada (1966, p. 112) saw this aspect of the problem very clearly, stating:

> The development of our film industry has always been hindered by difficulties found in markets with a solid film industry. These markets close their doors to a film industry that in time might become a competitor. These markets might accept an extraordinary film... but not our general production because they reserve the right to make films with standardized procedures and on an industrial basis, that are introduced in our theatres without difficulties. On the other hand, our films, not backed by a production of one hundred films per year, are rejected.

Godoy Quezada referred specifically to Argentina and Mexico, and concluded that foreign markets for Chilean films could only be found in other Latin American countries with film industries similar in size to Chile's. It is interesting to note that his view of the Argentine or Mexican cinematographies paralleled the view that an Argentine or Mexican "cinéaste" might have had vis-à-vis the U.S. or Western European cinematographies.

In 1942, CORFO published the operational basis for Chile Films; the state retained more than 50% of capital while the University of Chile and private investors shared the rest. Argentina Sono Films, the largest private film company in Argentina, was to provide commercial, administrative, and technical advice. But Argentina Sono Films exported its own model of studio organization and type of film to Chile, a model that attempted to replicate Hollywood, and that soon would prove unviable in Argentina itself.

The building of studios was initiated in October 1942, and concluded late in 1943. Excellent technical equipment was purchased in the United States, and the first production made by Chile Films was released in October 1944—an historical drama that found adverse critical reception. Chilean film production increased in the 1944–1947 period; World War II, the interruption in the flow of European films, and the economic policies of the Radical party governments created the conditions for this increase, which was the most pronounced in the history of Chilean sound films (Tables 3 and 10). The films exported to Mexico by Chile Films, however, were unsuccessful, and plans to export to the rest of the Latin America were subsequently abandoned. Several conflicts surrounded the administration of Chile Films, and there were opposing claims with regards to its economic viability. The problems were compounded by a lack of stability in its directive cadres, part of a bureaucratic structure too dependent on changes in the political atmosphere.[2]

By 1947, Chile Films began to follow a path similar to the one followed in Argentina at the time: imitate the "international style," attempting to reach middle-class audiences through the adaptation of the classics of world literature. Three films were made in 1948, although by this time Chile Films was heavily in debt, and its future viability was in serious doubt. Audiences became skeptical about local films, and avoided them. Middle class audiences saw their prejudices about local productions confirmed, and popular audiences saw their disposable incomes reduced and a renewed influx of Argentine and Mexican productions. Chile Films produced only one picture in 1949; released in 1950. This was the last CORFO production. The studios were then leased to private entrepreneurs that used them sporadically, subletting them for specific films. Film production languished until the mid-1960s.

It is worth noting that Chile Films, designed to promote film production both through its own films and servicing independent producers, was in competition with the studios owned by private capital,[3] and also that the commercial character of Chile Films remained unaltered throughout its existence. Film production remained intermittent, without a firm economic foundation; no adequate laws protecting local filmmaking existed.

Chilean filmmaking did not find new momentum until the early 1960s, under a radically changed political climate and based on radically different cultural assumptions and projects. Before concentrating on feature film production during the Frei (1964-1970) and Allende (1970-1973) governments, the following paragraphs present a brief review of political developments in the 1950s, and Chilean film producers' and directors' efforts to secure state support for local production in the 1940s and 1950s.

Ibañez del Campo became president in 1952 after defeating several candidates including Salvador Allende, presidential candidate for the So-

---

[2] Another member of the Radical Party, Gonzalez Videla, was elected president in 1946, with Communist party support. This alliance did not last and Gonzalez Videla soon outlawed Communist activity and froze workers' wages; massive discontent and government repression followed. It should be noted that, although disagreeing with the Conservatives, the Radicals, the dominant political party from 1938 to 1952, were part and parcel of a political system that in crucial moments always favored the interests of the hegemonic mercantile and financial groups in Chile.

[3] Besides Chile Films, two other studios operated in Chile in the era of sound. Chile Sono Films was founded in 1938 with equipment brought from Argentina. It changed hands in 1941 becoming VDB which made several films. Santa Elena studios were created in 1941, at the peak of World War II, and disappeared in 1948, after the stimulation created by the war ceased.

cialist party. Ibañez promised and attempted at first a populist course of action aimed at redistributing income and widening the scope of civil liberties. A new decline in international copper prices thwarted the project of income redistribution. Ibañez sought new loans from U.S. banks and the International Monetary Fund, while inflation and frozen wages reduced the purchasing power of the popular sector.

In 1958, the parties of the left formed an alliance, Frente de Acción Popular (FRAP, or Popular Action Front); Allende was FRAP's presidential candidate. Jorge Alessandri, candidate for the Conservative party and son of the former president, was elected over Allende by a relatively small number of votes. Alessandri's policies attempted to stimulate the economy through an increase in credit and allowing a freer play to direct foreign investment. Such investments were now channeled towards commerce and manufacturing industries: Chile had entered a dependency stage with new characteristics.[4] By 1962, however, foreign capital could not suffice to stimulate the nation's economy, and inflation and balance of payments problems returned.

DEFENSE OF THE CHILEAN FILM INDUSTRY

In 1944, the magazine *Ercilla* surveyed the opinion of Chilean filmmakers on measures needed to revitalize local production. The measures suggested by the filmmakers included the mandatory exhibition of Chilean films, elimination of taxes on celluloid and equipment, CORFO loans for independent producers, and a reciprocity law with countries that exported their films to Chile. By 1948, a Commission to Defend Chilean Cinema appealed to president Gonzalez Videla, who stated "Chile Films has not been a success but it can change its course, creating better conditions for local producers" (quoted in Godoy Quezada, 1966, p. 128). Chile Films, however, discontinued its operations in 1949. By 1953, neither the government nor local producers were interested in financing local films; Chile Films studios were closed and decaying. This situation prompted producers and directors to reorganize; in 1955 they created DIPROCINE, an organization aimed at promoting "initiatives and courses of action towards the establishment, development, and protection of a [national] film industry geared to the cultural demands and economic advantage of our coun-

---

[4] The "new character of dependency" has been pointed out by Cardoso and Faletto (1979, pp. 149–71). This stage involved the progressive internationalization of domestic Latin American markets. Multinational firms became interested in producing for the domestic markets where they usually chose monopolistic or oligopolistic branches of the economy and used protectionism to their own advantage.

try" (quoted in Ossa Coo, 1971, p. 69). DIPROCINE, however, did not achieve results quickly.

Film producers and directors continued with their activities to defend Chilean filmmaking. By the early 1960s, the main objective was to obtain a refund on state taxes levied at the box office, a refund that would be channeled towards local film production. No state support would be forthcoming, however, until the Christian Democratic party won the 1964 presidential elections.

FILM PRODUCTION IN CHILE, 1960–1980[5]

Chilean cinematography began to gain new momentum in the early 1960s, but this new momentum was often based on cultural premises that differed from previous attempts. These new cultural premises included: a. new production structures (universities, television, political parties, low-budget independent production with personal funds); b. new cultural forms, or cultural forms that were in the historical context of Chilean feature-length films (documentaries, semi-documentaries, and historical films reflecting a critical approach to Chilean history and society); c. the attempt to reach a new public besides the one reached through the commercial exhibition circuit: trade unions, progressive political parties, popular organizations, shanty towns residents. Although the new Chilean filmmakers did not reject commercial exhibition, they often found their products rejected by the commercial outlets.

What were the contextual aspects favoring the new film culture and film practice of the younger Chilean filmmakers? By the early 1960s, university students took a renewed interest in mass communication. The University of Chile was the site of the first *cineclub* (film society), organized in 1958. In the Catholic University, the Film Institute gathered young people interested in film as mass communication and as an instrument to assist social change. In 1960, the state university (University of Chile) created both the Department of Experimental Cinema and a *Cinemateca* (film archives). The Department of Experimental Cinema produced an important series of short documentaries and invited world-famous documentalist Joris Ivens to teach. Edgar Morin, French sociologist and one of the originators of "cinéma vérité," was also invited to teach in 1962. Established in 1962 under the control of the universities, television also pro-

---

[5] The basic bibliographic sources for this section are Ossa Coo (1971), Torres and Perez Estremera (1973), Chanan (1976), and Bolzoni (1974).

vided an important training ground for young filmmakers; several of them worked for the new medium. Last but not least, the Viña del Mar film festival, founded in 1962, provided an important meeting ground for Chilean and foreign filmmakers. In 1967, this festival organized the first meeting of new Latin American filmmakers. The above factors provided an important basis for the technical and cultural development of young filmmakers with new orientations towards the activity and revitalized local film production. As a result, more feature films and documentaries were produced under Frei's government (Tables 3 and 10).

Enjoying wholesale economic and political support from the U.S., the Christian Democrats had won the 1964 presidential elections. Frei, the Christian Democratic candidate, came to the presidency promising a "revolution in freedom" aimed at correcting the remarkable inequities in Chilean society while avoiding a process of violent class struggle (Keen and Wasserman, 1980, p. 340). "Chilenization" (an alternative to nationalization of the all important copper industry), a moderate agrarian reform, and tax reforms, were the mainstays of his economic program designed to stimulate industrial growth and redistribute income to the popular sectors. By the end of 1965, however, wages were again frozen in an effort to attract more foreign and domestic investment, and redistributive efforts ceased. Inflation returned to erode the popular sector's income, and the agrarian reform progressed slowly. The above factors favored a renewed radicalization of industrial workers; urban slum dwellers and rural workers organized for the first time.

Frei's government implemented several measures designed to foster local film production, attempting simultaneously to control and redirect the most radicalized activities in the medium. These measures included the creation of a Council for the Promotion of the Film Industry (staffed mostly by bureaucrats), duty free importation of raw film and equipment, prizes for quality productions and, most important, a 1967 protectionist law establishing that box office taxes be reimbursed to local producers. The Christian Democratic government support measures included the creation of Continental Films, a mixed capital distribution company in charge of distributing Chilean films under terms advantageous to local producers. Overall, government support for Chilean films resembled its partial nationalization of copper mines and its agrarian reform, in that it attempted to reform current practices without basically affecting fundamental interests. In the area of filmmaking, the above course of action meant emphasizing supportive protectionist measures without affecting distribution and exhibition commercial practices or the hegemonic presence of foreign distributors.

The above measures created, nonetheless, a more propitious atmosphere for local film production and the films released began to explore more of Chilean societal problems. The number of films produced grew from four in 1966 to ten in 1968, although some of these were documentaries rejected by the commercial exhibition circuits. A 1967 fictional film was also rejected by distributors and exhibitors due to its ideological content. The film, Helvio Soto's *Erase un Niño, un Guerrillero y un Caballo* (A Child, a Guerrilla, and a Horse), was later exhibited for one week, but the incident made clear that distributors and exhibitors were not influenced only by commercial considerations. The 1969 film *Caliche Sangriento* (Blood Stained Mineral), a film that took an historical revision line of enquiry, exploring the economic causes of Chile's 1879 war against Peru, was banned by the Censorship Board. The indignant reaction of various groups helped lift the prohibition and the film was finally exhibited.

By 1968, the opposition between old style *folklorista* films and new tendencies was clearer, as some Chilean films began to reflect the lives and problems of wider sectors of the population. Filmmaking felt the impact of the mobilization and organization of popular sectors for the 1970 elections that brought Allende to the presidency. A group of young film directors attempted to align their productions with the new *Unidad Popular* (Popular Unity) coalition being formed in the political arena. During Allende's campaign, these filmmakers formed a Committee to Support Popular Unity and took their films to trade unions, schools, slums, and open air meetings, reaching a wider audience than in commercial theatres.[6] The practice of showing a film followed by political discussion marked a radical departure from the previous exclusively commercial use of the medium.

The Allende Years, 1970–1973

Salvador Allende was elected president in 1970 as the candidate of Unidad Popular (UP), a leftist coalition of Socialists, Communists, and radicalized fractions of the Radical and Christian Democratic parties. Allende took office in an atmosphere of optimism and expectation, and many felt that UP's program of far reaching socioeconomic reforms had a chance to initiate a non-violent process of transition toward socialism. Popular Unity's government project was to initiate Chile's transition toward socialism by strengthening, extending, and streamlining the extant mechanisms for state intervention in the economy devised by sectors of the country's political elite to stimulate the economy following the 1930 economic depression. In the area of film-related activities the above strategy meant the coexistence of a state and a private sector; Chile Films, always a state company, was the government's main resource.

[6] Commercially released, these films would never have reached an audience of more than a few thousand spectators. Miguel Littin's film *El Chacal de Nahueltoro* (Nahueltoro Jackal) was an exception; it reached 500,000 spectators in commercial theatres and many others in shows organized in political parties' premises and other similar non-theatrical settings. Most of the innovative films made between 1968 and 1971 were made outside the formal mechanisms of Chile Films and its distributor Continental Films.

The UP coalition supported a program of progressive nationalization of large foreign companies and domestic oligopolies in banking, commerce, and industry, and the expropriation and redistribution of all landholdings over 80 hectares. In Congress, UP could count on the support of the Christian Democrats' left wing. The domestic and international forces pitted against Allende's government, however, were formidable, including the Chilean judiciary and most of the military ranking officers, the domestic economic establishment, and the foreign interests and multinational companies. Anti-UP forces controlled most of Chile's mass media (Fagen, 1974).

The first years of UP rule saw a remarkable increase in workers' wages and purchasing power and a massive program of public spending aimed at boosting social services and reducing unemployment. Price controls were imposed. These and similar measures stimulated economic activity, curbed unemployment, and improved the popular sector's living standards. But a sharp decline in international copper prices coincided with the expropriation of the most important copper mines in July 1971, a move that interrupted the flow of U.S. private investment capital and ended the credit from such agencies as the Export-Import Bank or the Agency for International Development (AID). Stagnation and inflation returned to plague the Chilean economy, while farmers and medium-size businessmen became less willing to cooperate with the UP government.

By the end of 1972, the Allende administration faced an advanced economic and political crisis. Besides the disruptions that usually accompany every process of far reaching social change, and the mistakes and conflicts within the governing coalition, the economic chaos was fostered by large domestic and international economic interests. The opposition expected to attain a major victory in the March 1973, congressional elections, but was disappointed to see the UP vote rise, a clear sign of popular support for Allende's policies of income redistribution and full employment. When electoral means failed the powerful international and domestic interests that opposed Allende renewed their pressure on the military forces to intervene. A premature and unsuccessful military coup in June 1973, was followed by another one on September 10 that overthrew the UP government. Allende rejected a demand that he resign, and was killed in the army and air force attack on the presidential palace.

Film Policies under Allende

At the time when Allende came to the presidency, distribution of about 80% of the films shown in Chile was in the hands of the large U.S.-based companies, and 95% of the films shown on television were from the United States. Thirty-one first-run theatres were located in Santiago, 27 of which were under the control of two financial groups; similar groups controlled exhibition in the interior. Twelve distribution companies were in operation, eight of which were branches of U.S. companies. Insofar as UP tactics relied on the utilization and expansion of existing state organisms Chile Films remained the main element of the government's film policy. The director of *El Chacal de Nahueltoro,* Miguel Littin, was appointed head of Chile Films. Littin stated: "Chile Films should be the basis for the organization of the Chilean Institute of Cinematographic Art and Industry. Such an institution should produce our own films and transform film into the vanguard of national culture" (quoted in Torres and Perez Estremera, 1973, p. 112).

Several Chile Films problems, however, proved themselves difficult to correct. Its equipment was by now outdated and its bureaucrats could not be removed because of the "Democratic Guarantees" that Allende was forced to sign before assuming the country's presidency. Each of the political parties in the UP coalition followed somewhat different strategies and courses of action, a fact that was reflected by the change in Chile Films' head officers. Littin was replaced after 10 months in office; the new Chile Films director reoriented the activity away from feature films and towards less costly documentaries. By October 1972, about 30 documentaries were at different stages of completion. The diffusion of Chile Films' documentaries, however, was partially blocked by the persistence of private commercial structures in the distribution and exhibition sectors. Social and political documentaries could be shown on television and through the above mentioned non-traditional outlets, but did not have access to the privately-owned theatres.

On July 11, 1971, the most important U.S.-owned copper mines were nationalized and Washington retaliated by blocking loans and credit. The U.S.-based film distributors stopped exporting features to Chile and joined in destabilizing the market by demanding that small exhibitors make advance payments for film rentals. The most conservative press complained about the shortage of films. At the beginning of 1972, all the U.S.-based distributors were operating through reissues, and their Santiago offices were under government intervention. As Ehrmann explained, "one reason for this could well be an apprehension that, if left on their own, the companies might destroy prints of their earlier releases, intensifying shortage of products here" (Ehrmann, 1973).

Approximately 180 new films were released in Chile during 1972, a 40% reduction via-a-vis 1971, but audiences increased due to the low admissions charged. The void created by the absence of U.S. films was to a large extent filled with French, Italian, Mexican, and Argentine productions. The production of Chilean feature films was slower than anticipated: two were released in 1972, but early in 1973 seven were at the completion stage, and three others were in process, two of them relatively expensive historical films produced by Chile Films.

The state-owned distribution company, a branch of Chile Films, imported close to 25% of the films released in 1972, mostly from France and the socialist countries. Chile Films had created a national distribution agency aimed at taking over one-third of the 300 films to be imported annually (300 films was the annual importation quota approved by the Central Bank). Allende's government objective in the area of film distribution was to achieve a division of the market in three equal shares: one-third for the state, one-third for private independent distributors, and one-third for the large U.S. companies affiliated with the Motion Picture Export Association.

For the U.S.-based companies, used to handling close to 80% of film imports, the above policy, much milder than complete nationalization of film distribution, was still a drastic step, a reduction in control from 80 to 33% of film imports. But for national independent distributors, used to importing 20% of the films shown in Chile, it was a distinct improvement (from 20 to 33% of the market), made even more attractive by their access to official foreign exchange rates.

As distributor, Chile Films' objectives were to import selected films from the U.S., Western Europe, the socialist countries, and the Third World film movement. Bilateral film exchange pacts were signed with Bulgaria, Cuba, Hungary, and Czechoslovakia. By 1972, Chile Films owned only one theatre in Santiago but aimed to expand its exhibition facilities into a network. The need to expand was based on the fact that in many cases private cinema owners refused to show the films handled by the state distribution agency, and this rivalry was not only commercial but also politico-ideological, as the important theatre owners had several links with the private banking sector (Lopez, 1972). Chile Films' project was to create an exhibition network to exhibit films followed by political discussion, and it was thought that such a network could at first be based on the few theatres directly owned by banks and other nationalized companies. The long term goal was to transform these theatres into peoples' cultural centers, a project requiring time and financial resources (Bolzoni, 1974, p. 56). This project was interrupted in September 1973, by the military coup that overthrew the Popular Unity government.[7] The coup introduced deep changes in Chile's model of socio-economic development and drastically interrupted the momentum in local filmmaking that began in the early 1960s.

After the 1973 coup, Chile experienced one of the greatest large-scale operations of repression in Latin American history. Under the new military

---

[7] Several mechanisms that throughout this book have been considered "normal" in film-related institutions in capitalist-dependent countries were not operative in Chile during 1973. Admission prices were extremely low, but the Allende government was reluctant to raise them. The Censorship Board functioned with a minimum of members as the government had refused to confirm the censors proposed by the Universities and the parents' associations. In this transition period censorship lost its customary function of preventing the presentation of oppositional ideologies in film; only two films (both of the soft-porn variety) were banned in Chile in 1973 before the September military coup.

government civil liberties were abolished, the national congress dissolved, all union activities banned, the agrarian and economic reforms erased. The junta's program of restoring the free market froze wages instead of prices, but inflation did not decline, and unemployment rose sharply. Large industrial and agricultural holdings were returned to the private sector, and foreign multinational corporations, some of which had been expropriated by Unidad Popular, returned to Chile. Such policies produced renewed income concentration. A plesbicite held in January 1978, apparently boosted the military government intentions of remaining in power for an extended period of time.

Chilean Film Production after September, 1973

A very active movement of Chilean filmmaking in exile began in 1974, and at least sixteen feature films were made between 1974 and 1979. In contrast, very few feature films have been made in Chile under the military government, and the communications and filmmaking schools remain closed. Four films can be mentioned, of which only one (*Julio comienza en Julio* (Julio begins in July), produced and directed by Silvio Caiozzi) has been shown commercially, with moderate success. This film was released commercially in April 1979, and presented at the Cannes film festival. Inaugurating a mechanism that might facilitate somewhat the release of other (future) films, Catholic University sponsorship has allowed this film to be free of state taxes during the first three months of exhibition (Vega, 1979, p. 48).

The above overview of the evolution of filmmaking and state protectionist policies in Chile is intended as a case study of the specific situation of local filmmaking in medium-size Latin American countries.[8]

The evolution of state protection and independent filmmaking in Chile also makes it apparent that state protectionist policies towards local cinema are guided not only by economic but also by politico-ideological considerations. In the next chapter, the case of Bolivia will support this contention, and also provides an instance of the possibilities and problems of national filmmaking in a small market Latin American nation.

[8] It should be noted that the paucity of national film production in Chile after the September, 1973 coup seems to reflect the specifics of the politico-cultural situation there more than an inherent characteristic of medium-size market, Latin American countries. Two other such countries, Colombia and Venezuela, have experienced promising increments in national film production in the 1970s. In both countries the growth in national film production was spurred by the implementation of supportive protectionist policies.

Chapter 7
Filmmaking in Bolivia, 1930–1981[1]

Landlocked Bolivia provides a case for examining the possibilities and limits of feature film production in a small-market Latin American country.[2] The case of Bolivia also shows that, although completely backward from an industrial point of view, film production in a small-market developing country can attain a cultural importance that does not correspond to its economic infrastructure. In part, this cultural importance has been enhanced by the fact that beginning in the early 1960s, some of the most important Bolivian films successfully challenged the medium's dominant mode of use, going beyond the commercial theatre circuits and reaching the popular sectors through alternative circuits initiated by trade unions and political groups.

The Bolivian film market is small, not only because there are relatively fewer inhabitants than in Argentina, Brazil, or Chile, but also because of low income levels severely maldistributed, relatively low industrialization

[1] Unless otherwise noted, this chapter's information is based on Gumucio Dragón (1981), Hennessey (1968), Klein (1979), Mesa Gisbert (1976, 1979), Sanjinés (1979), and Weil et al. (1974).

[2] The notion of market size itself should be submitted to scrutiny, as it is intimately bound with modes of production and their articulation in specific social formations; such articulation finds expression in income distribution structures. Market size is then overdetermined by income distribution, plus specific historical and cultural characteristics, and is also related to the nature of film as cultural product and the dominant definition of its use. Throughout this book the size of the Latin American domestic markets for film is considered as actual size given actual conditions, as opposed to potential market according to unmet demand.

and urbanization, and the extreme cultural gap among the country's social and ethnic groups, divided among a minority white population of European ancestry, a large group of bilingual "mestizos", and a majority indigenous population that in many cases has maintained its original language and several features of its original culture.[3] If we add to the above an extreme case of political instability, it is understandable that local film production found it extremely difficult to establish a beachhead for the viable production of feature films.

Another characteristic of film activities in small-market countries, is that these activities are usually circumscribed to a small circle of filmmakers. Consequently, the present chapter offers a more detailed and individualized account of these activities.

We have seen in Chapter 6 that filmmaking in the era of silent film in a medium-sized market country like Chile did not differ very much from the structure of similar activities in the larger countries (Argentina, Brazil, and Mexico). In countries more isolated and with smaller markets, like Bolivia, however, local filmmaking was much more restricted from the very beginning. Isolation and a smaller potential market presented more obstacles and fewer incentives for attempting to overcome the technological gap with advanced countries. The first film show, for instance, took place in 1909, a full 14 years after the first film shows in the largest and less isolated Latin American countries. But even facing such severe restrictive conditions, toward the end of the silent era Bolivian filmmaking began to show signs of enthusiastic activity.

Although a 1925 film is usually considered the first Bolivian feature film, an earlier film was *La Profecía del Lago* (The Lake's Prophecy) made in 1923. It was banned by the authorities on the day of its premiere for, among other things, presenting an interracial and inter-class love story (white upper-class woman/Indian lower-class man). From the very beginning, filmmaking in Bolivia could not ignore the realities of a large, marginalized Indian population, a trend that also found expression in the *indigenista* movement in literature. The fate of this first Bolivian feature makes apparent that this approach did not bid well for the relations with censors. This film was made about nine years later than first features in the larger countries.

Corazón Aymará (Aymara Heart) made in 1925 by the Italian immigrant Pedro Sambarino, is usually regarded as the first Bolivian feature film. *Wara-Wara* (1929), and *Hacia la Gloria* (Towards Glory) (1931), close the brief cycle of silent feature films made in these years. These last two features attracted a good number of viewers, and *Wara-Wara*, a romantic story set near the end of the Inca empire, also enjoyed critical success.

---

[3] Indian population is estimated at 60% of the population, "mestizo" about 33%, the rest white (see Weil et al., 1974, pp. 77-98).

From a commercial point of view, however, both films saw their chances of recovering their investments curtailed by the introduction of foreign sound films. From this point on, Bolivia would witness the familiar pattern of numerically limited upper and middle classes preferring American and European films, and other sectors of the population (also numerically limited to white and mestizo lower-class sectors) consuming mostly Argentinian and some Mexican "talkies." Insofar as most of the indigenous population had meager if any cash incomes and did not speak Spanish, they had a very limited exposure to the medium. The first attempts to make fully sonorized feature-length movies would have to wait until the success of the 1952 nationalist revolution.

THE 1930s DECADE: GREEN HELL

The early 1930s, when a transition to sound film production could have been attempted, were marked by the Chaco War between Bolivia and Paraguay, the result of a conflict that had been simmering for several years. The 1930s international economic depression, and the Chaco war resulted in very poor conditions to attempt risky enterprises in Bolivia.

The early years of the 1920s had seen a remarkable post-World War I recovery for the Bolivian tin mining industry, which led to its highest production figures by 1929. This enormous output, however, coincided with a long-term trend of steady international price decline, a trend that continued long after the 1930s depression. By 1930, there was a serious crisis in the international tin market, and Bolivian national income suffered a pronounced decline. The year 1930 saw the last major capital investment in tin mining; thereafter the Bolivian industry would produce at even higher costs.

Daniel Salamanca, a Cochabamba landowner and leader of a fraction of the Republican Party[4] had become president in 1930. Facing deep cuts in national income, Salamanca attempted to take new economic measures but ran into the opposition of the middle classes and the Liberal Party, his main political allies. A long-standing border conflict led Salamanca to declare war against Paraguay against the advice of the General Staff.

Raging from 1932 to 1935 the Chaco War, a conflict over mostly uninhabited and poorly demarcated Chaco Boreal territory, was a long and costly disaster for Bolivia. Many men and much more territory than was originally in dispute were lost. An unintended effect of the war was that it eroded the extant white/Indian caste system, as high-plateau Indians, conscripted to fight in the tropical jungles, refused upon demobilization to

[4] The Republican Party had been organized in 1914 by white and upper middle class politicians with a fundamental belief in liberal and positivist ideologies.

return to their former servitude. Migrating to towns, many became politicized and provided an important part of the mass base for new revolutionary parties and for a militant trade unionism (Hennessy, 1968).

In other social sectors, among young and literate war veterans, the war frustrations originated the so-called Chaco generation. Believing that traditional politicians influenced by international oil companies had led to a disastrous war, returning veterans set up Socialist and radical parties willing to challenge the traditional political system. This atmosphere of unrest resulted in the overthrow of the civilian government, and the first advent of military rule in Bolivia since 1880. Younger nationalist and progressive army officers seized the government in 1936, inaugurating a period of "military socialism" marked by relatively unsuccessful attempts to reform Bolivian society from above (Col. David Toro from 1936 to 1937, and Major German Busch from 1937 to 1939). These governments attempted to weaken the power of the landholding and mining oligarchy, but the most important landmarks of the military socialism years were the confiscation of Standard Oil holdings in Bolivia, the creation of an important labor code, and the writing, in 1938, of a socially advanced constitution. These progressive military governments were replaced by a more conservative one in 1939.

The only feature-length film made and released during these years was *Infierno Verde* (Green Hell), a documentary on the Chaco war made by Luis Bazoberry, one of the local filmmakers, that recorded episodes of that war on film. Bazoberry had edited this film in Spain and had added a sound track incorporating narration and music. This film was thus midway between a silent and a synchronous sound film, and can be considered either as the last important film of the silent era, or a precedent for future filmmaking activities. Released in 1938, it is the only documentary on the Chaco war made public in Bolivia. It was exhibited in La Paz for a long time.

NEW POLITICAL GROUPS:
THE 1940s DECADE

World War II found Bolivia producing tin for the U.S. at so-called solidarity prices, while nationalist and socialist political forces that took form during the Chaco War organized into new political parties. The civilian dissident groups began to organize themselves into opposition parties of national importance. Of these, the most important were the middle class and initially fascist-inclined MNR, and the Marxist Partido de la Izquierda Revolucionaria (Revolutionary Left Party). Both groups were well represented in the national Congress of 1940–1944. The Nationalist Revolutionary Movement (Movimiento Nacionalista Revolucionario, MNR) supported in 1943 a coup that inaugurated a new and short-lived progressive period.

This coup deposed the elected president, Gen. Peñaranda, and the new military rulers attempted an innovative government in alliance with the MNR. Col. Villarroel (1943–1946) accomplished little, with the exception of an initial mobilization of Indian peasants by the MNR. In 1946, Villarroel was overthrown and killed in a bloody revolution. During the next six years (1946–1952) the traditional political parties returned to the foreground.

The only filming activity during the 1940s was the work of two amateurs, Jorge Ruiz and Augusto Roca, who made 8mm films. They became professionals in 1947 when, in association with a U.S. citizen living in Bolivia, they founded Bolivia Films, a company that produced the first sonorized Bolivian short in 1948, and made several documentaries and other films in the following years.

NATIONALISM AND SOCIAL REFORM, 1952–1964

The MNR won the 1951 presidential election, but the military intervened and formed a military junta government. Deprived of its election victory the MNR launched several unsuccessful revolts, until in April 1952, it overthrew the military regime. In the process, the MNR disassociated itself from its fascist wing, and sought an alliance with miners' trade unions; Lechín, a popular miners' labor leader, entered the MNR.

The generalized insurrection led the MNR to take power with the support of miners and peasants. Several progressive measures were taken: nationalization of mines, agrarian reform, universal franchise, and nationalization of several foreign companies. Workers, civilians, students, and peasants were armed, and the conservatively-oriented army was dismantled. Thus began the Bolivian National Revolution, one of the most important social revolutions in Latin America. In October 1952, the three biggest tin-mining companies were nationalized, and August 1953, saw a far reaching land reform decree. Indian peasants were granted land, were freed from servile labor obligations, were allowed to vote, and received large supplies of arms. From then on, Indian peasants became a factor in Bolivian politics.

Most MNR reforms were implemented under the momentum of the first years of the Nationalist government, during the presidency of Paz Estenssoro (1952–1956). Siles Suazo (1956–1960) attempted a more conservative course of bringing runaway inflation under control with massive financial support from the U.S. During Siles' administration the scope of most of the previous advanced social measures was severely reduced, and U.S. oil companies were invited back to Bolivia for the first time since the 1937 Standard Oil confiscation.

Paz Estenssoro returned to the Presidency in 1960, but instead of reinstating social reforms, he consolidated his predecessor's more conservative course of action. Concurrently, the power of the army was being revived with U.S. support. When Paz Estenssoro initiated a new term in office his weakened and splintered MNR government was overthrown by the military in 1964. The MNR's populism and ambiguity in its final years opened the door to a new militarism.

The April 1952, nationalist revolution also had consequences for the institutions of cultural production. In the area of film, this can be seen in the creation of the Bolivian Film Institute, with the double mission of encouraging the growth and development of new filmmakers and using film as an instrument for people's advancement, education, and consciousness raising. In July 1952, a Department of Cinematography was created as part of the Press and Propaganda Ministry. This Department was the basis for the creation of the *Instituto Cinematográfico Boliviano* (Bolivian Film Institute) created one year later. The Institute became an important site for the development of technical personnel. Although its main productions were newsreels and documentaries, the Institute provided firmer foundations for future film experiences.

The Bolivian Film Institute was one of the main components of the MNR government's propaganda apparatus (the Institute undertook the production of many documentaries and newsreels publicizing the government actions), but also became the first step towards a national cinematography, allowing young filmmakers new experiences backed by better technical and economic means. The work of the Bolivian Film Institute was more remarkable during the enthusiastic momentum of Paz Estenssoro's first administration, and almost 200 newsreels were made between 1953 and 1956. Besides newsreels, more than 400 shorts were made between 1952 and 1962.

Jorge Ruiz was the most significant Bolivian filmmaker in the period from 1945 to 1960. Ruiz associated with Augusto Roca to found Bolivia Films, a company that had an important role in filmmaking in the 1950s, producing a large number of documentaries. The new social, political, and cultural conditions created by the first MNR government brought an upsurge of optimism that gave new momentum to local filmmaking. By the end of 1952, Ruiz and other filmmakers began the first attempt to make a commercial feature film in Bolivia, *Detrás de los Andes* (Beyond the Andes), that was left unfinished because of financial difficulties. (Part of this material was used by Ruiz many years later in his 1969 release *Mina Alaska*.) If finished, it would have become the first fully sonorized Bolivian feature film.

These years also saw the beginning of a handful of small production companies geared to the production of documentaries and other non-fiction films commissioned either by the Bolivian government or by agencies of the U.S. government. (U.S. financial and technical assistance became an important source of support for the MNR government after 1956.)

The two most ambitious films of the 1950s decade were directed by Ruiz. *Vuelve Sebastiana* (Sebastiana, Return!) was a semi-documentary, anthropological film focused on a tribe of Chipaya Indians, a group with distinct language and culture but increasingly integrated into the *"Aymara"* culture. This film was awarded the first prize for ethnographic films in the 1953 Montevideo international festival.

Three years later, in 1956, Ruiz became the Bolivian Film Institute technical director, and continued his work as a filmmaker. Relying now on state support, Ruiz was able to direct, in 1958, the first Bolivian feature film with sound: *La Vertiente* (The Waterfall). This feature-length semi-documentary combined a love story with a background provided by a real-life rural community struggling to secure a source of safe drinking water. Though a fictional story, this film presented the ideas of solidarity, community effort, and integrated development, reflecting in a fashion the U.S. aid to the Siles government, such aid being at the time framed within an ideology of self-reliant community development. After these films, Ruiz continued his filmmaking career, both in Bolivia and abroad.[5]

While Ruiz was the most important filmmaker throughout the 1950s, Jorge Sanjinés played that role during the 1960s, and Antonio Eguino throughout the 1970s. Both Sanjinés' and Eguino's careers, however, unfolded under military regimes brought about by the 1964 overthrow of the MNR government, when, supported by conservative elements and the peasants, Gen. Barrientos seized the government and dissolved most of the organized labor opposition. From 1964 to 1969, Barrientos led a process of conservative economic reform and political demobilization of all popular groups except the peasants. It was under his government that the army fought with guerrillas led by Che Guevara. These years also saw the organization of the Ukamau group.

THE UKAMAU GROUP

As mentioned above, the 1952 nationalist revolution had had a profound effect on a new generation of Bolivian intellectuals. The 12 years of nationalist government (1952–1964) gave new possibilities to film directors to learn their craft through documentaries and other short films commissioned by or made within the context of the Bolivian Film Institute. The

---

[5] Bolivian author Gumucio Dragón (1981, p. 77) remarked that most of Ruiz films were financed by the MNR government, by U.S. agencies, or by the Alliance for Progress. He has made few independent films, *Vuelve Sebastiana* being one of the few.

importance of the role played by the Institute in these years can be seen, in that almost all the filmmakers active from 1952 on were at one point or another related to its activities, and the filmmakers of the Ukamau group were not an exception.

Sanjinés can be considered an intellectual outgrowth of the 1952 generation. After studying both film and philosophy for two years in Chile (from 1958 to 1960), Jorge Sanjinés returned to Bolivia where he engaged in several projects with scriptwriter Oscar Soria.[6] They founded a film society, and created a short-lived film school. In 1961, they made their first film, a semi-documentary commissioned by a government agency. It is, however, the 1963 short *Revolución* (Revolution) that first showed Sanjinés' interest in probing film as a critical instrument capable of stimulating viewers' critical reflection on the country's problems. Finished shortly before the 1964 military coup, this short uses only images and music to present a powerful exploration of underdevelopment, class struggle, and the 1952 nationalist insurrection.

By 1964, the conservative sectors of the army had coalesced and reorganized. A military coup overthrew the by then splintered and discredited MNR government, installing General Barrientos in the presidency. Miners' salaries were reduced and their protest met with severe repression both in May and September, 1965. Ironically, the Barrientos government (1964–1969) gave Sanjinés the opportunity to become the Bolivian Film Institute technical director and make his first feature film: *Ukamau*, a film made between 1964 and 1965 and released in 1966.[7] *Ukamau* (meaning "it is like this" in the *Aymará* language) was the first feature film spoken in *Aymará*.[8] It is very important to stress the contextual importance of a film spoken in *Aymará*, the first Bolivian film that could be directly understood by Indian audiences, but required Spanish sub-titles for Spanish-speaking audiences.

Through a relatively simple story of assasination and revenge, this film exposed the existing domination among the various socio-ethnic sectors of the Bolivian highlands (*"altiplano"*). *Ukamau*, released in 1966, presented a clear picture of social stratification in the Bolivian *"altiplano"* and the economic and cultural oppression of the Indian population. The release of this film and its favorable reception in Europe, where it was awarded the critics prize for young directors at the Cannes Festival,

[6] Telecine, a private film production company founded in 1954 was the training ground of Oscar Soria, scriptwriter of all of Sanjinés films made in Bolivia, and after that of both of Eguino's films (*Pueblo Chico* and *Chuquiago*).

[7] Under Sanjinés direction (1965–1968) the Institute produced 27 newsreels, four documentaries, a medium-length feature (*Aysa*) and a full-length feature film (*Ukamau*).

[8] It should be remembered that between 60 and 70% of the Bolivian population is more fluent in either one of the two major Indian languages (*Aymará* and *Quechua*) than in Spanish.

prompted the Barrientos government to demand Sanjinés' resignation. The Bolivian Film Institute was not only closed down but permanently dissolved, thus ending the Institute's role as a training ground for young Bolivian filmmakers.[9]

From this point on Sanjinés undertook an independent career, with experiences similar to those of several filmmakers in other parts of Latin America, experiences of a middle-class intellectual who turns to film as a way of exposing the oppressed peoples' condition, searching for an appropriate language and, whenever possible, a mode of film distribution and consumption that will bring the film to all popular sectors, not only to the usual audiences of critical films: radicalized students and intellectuals.

Sanjinés, Soria, and Rada created a production company, Ukamau Ltd., and Antonio Eguino joined them for the production of *Yaguar Mallku* (Blood of the Condor), a feature film this time spoken in Quechua. (The usual division of labor within the group at this time was: Sanjinés as director, Rada as executive producer, Soria as scriptwriter, and Eguino as cinematographer.) *Yaguar Mallku* is a complex film, that depicts, not only the contradictions among social groups and classes, and between urban and rural environments, but also focuses on the Peace Corps activities and population control in Indian communities. This film can also be considered the first feature-length independent production since the ones undertaken near the end of the silent era (independent in the sense of not being sponsored either by a Bolivian state agency or a U.S. government agency). Premiered in July 17, 1969, the government attempted to block its release, but massive demonstrations in La Paz and the support of students and intellectual groups removed this obstacle. *Yaguar Mallku* was finally exhibited, not only in the cities, but also in mines and rural centers, where Indian peasants and miners gathered to discuss the film's content. The film was widely seen both in Bolivia and abroad, won several international awards, and became one of the outstanding examples of the New Latin American Cinema movement (see Burton, 1978).

Two more films were begun by the Ukamau group in Bolivia with Sanjinés as director: *Los Caminos de la Muerte* (Roads to Death), and *El Coraje del Pueblo* (People's Courage). These films were made under political conditions very different and much more favorable than the previous ones, but before these films were released, the consequences of a new right-wing military coup precluded Sanjinés from any further work in Bolivia. The death of Barrientos in 1969 had brought General Ovando to the government, signaling a new trend of nationalist orientation for a section of the military, an orientation similar to that of the Peruvian military at the time. As a highly visible measure, Ovando nationalized the Bolivian

---

[9] The Institute's equipment and valuable archives were later transferred to Bolivian Television.

interests of Gulf Oil Co. This brief renewal of social revolutionary and nationalist tendencies among part of the Bolivian military gained further momentum when Ovando was replaced by General Torres, who presided over a radicalization of Ovando's orientation. In August 1971, however, his government was overthrown by a rightist army coup led by Col. Banzer, who from 1971 to 1978 presided over a dictatorial regime that welcomed foreign investment, and brought repression and censorship back to the foreground. Banzer's government benefitted from massive U.S. aid that helped overcome growing popular opposition.

Of the two films made by Sanjinés during the brief period of progressive military rule (1969–1971), one was left unfinished due to severe on-site and technical problems, and the second one was completed abroad after the 1971 coup. *Los Caminos de la Muerte*, began by the Ukamau group in 1970, was left unfinished, and most of its footage was ruined in a strange accident at a German processing laboratory. In 1971, Italian television (RAI) offered Sanjinés the possibility of making a new film, and Sanjinés chose *El Coraje del Pueblo*, centered on the government's repression and killing of miners in June 1967. This film was made under conditions of widespread popular mobilization and the incipient organization of institutions of popular political power. But the Banzer military coup that removed Torres from office in August 1971, took place when this film had just finished shooting, and the film editing was completed abroad.[10]

El Coraje del Pueblo (1971) centered on the denunciation of specific historical events more than on a fictional story. This film focused on the repeated massacres of miners by the army and police since 1942, culminating in the San Juan 1967 killing. Many of the actors were miners who had lived through the dramatic events recounted, and this fact lends a very direct impact to both image and sound. The director attempted a less paternalistic approach to the film's content, insofar as part of the intended audience also participated in the creation of the film.

After directing this film Sanjinés was not allowed to return to the Bolivia of the Banzer government, and the film was never openly exhibited in the country. This film closed the cycle of Sanjinés' films made in Bolivia, although he continued working, first in Peru and later in Ecuador. Sanjinés formed a new Ukamau group in exile, and in 1973 directed *El Enemigo Principal* (The Main Enemy) in Peru. In 1976, in co-production with the Central University at Quito, Ecuador, Sanjinés made *Fuera de Aquí* (Out of Here!), an overview of peasant's struggles in the Andean *altiplano*, and the multiple aspects of U.S. intervention in this struggle.

---

[10] Before the rightist military coup of 1971, new filmmakers working for Bolivian television had made some documentaries about various pressing social problems.

Both films were the result of teamwork, made directly within peasant communities, and intended as instruments of analysis and discussion in peasant communities and organizations. Deepening his previous orientation toward film as an arm of struggle, Sanjinés attempted to breach the gap with his intended audience (Indian peasants and miners) by incorporating not only their language but also a film form adequate to the purpose (Sanjinés, 1979). The film language employed eliminated all close-ups, attempting to adopt a mode of representation in accordance with the community as social and political actor, as different from the individual as actor.

His films have also attempted to go beyond international festivals, urban circles, and radicalized students and intellectuals, to be exhibited for and discussed by peasants, miners, and other popular sectors. In many cases, however, authoritarian regimes in Latin America have made it very difficult and dangerous to distribute these and other similarly oriented political films.

BOLIVIAN FILMMAKING IN THE DECADE OF THE 1970s

The 1971 military coup that installed Banzer in power created an extremely difficult situation for anyone interested in making films with clear ideological oppositional content, and even more for anyone interested in the wide diffusion and discussion of such films among popular sectors. The coup marked a turning point, signaling that the members of the Ukamau group would follow different courses of action.

El Coraje del Pueblo closed the cycle of Sanjinés' films made in Bolivia. This however, did not signal the demise of the Ukamau group in Bolivia. Eguino, who in 1969 had directed a short on the nationalization of Bolivian oil, and who had been the cinematographer of the Sanjinés movies, remained in Bolivia and followed a line of filmmaking that searched for a compromise with the extant political situation and its reflection in the Bolivian Censorship Board.

Facing an alternative of either exile or silence, Eguino chose a third alternative; making films that could be tolerated by the Bolivian Censorship Board, considering that Sanjinés' films were banned, and no parallel distribution was feasible. Antonio Eguino had joined the Ukamau group in 1967, after several years of study in the U.S., and did the cinematography of *Yaguar Mallcu* (Blood of the Condor). Commissioned by the Ovando government, in 1969 he directed *Basta,* a short on the nationalization of Gulf Oil interests in Bolivia. In 1973 Eguino directed his first feature film

Pueblo Chico (Small Village), released in 1974. Centered on the problems of a student who returns to his native village after studying abroad, this film depicted the village's social conditions and contradictions, and the dilemmas of a middle-class student who identifies with the problems of the Indian population in a social milieu that opposes the Indians' full participation in society. Several problems are present in the content of *Pueblo Chico:* racial conflicts, the deficiencies of formal education in the Bolivian countryside, and the institutionalized corruption of authorities and some peasant leaders. Attempting to integrate a social critique and a love story, the film sought a new path for Bolivian filmmaking, incorporating clear elements of social criticism and a somewhat general and abstract call to both reflection and action so as to avoid censorship under a very repressive cultural and political atmosphere. Its film form attempted to reflect reality more than to operate as an immediate instrument of popular debate and mobilization. Although the story is located in the countryside, the film itself is directed to urban audiences, as opposed to the previous Ukamau films.

Eguino's second feature, *Chuquiago* (made in 1977) continued the above line; it is a film of social critique framed within a very general progressive stance. *Chuquiago* is the first film made by the group that is focused on the urban milieu, facilitating the identification process of urban viewers. It is a bitter view of aspiration and desperation in various social strata of La Paz, Bolivia's most important city. Its four main characters typify the behavior and problems of various urban sectors: marginalized shanty-town dwellers, industrial workers, government bureaucrats, and the upper classes.

Both of Eguino's films, and especially the second, attracted an unprecedented number of viewers. *Chuquiago* was a very successful film, in the context of a market of this size. Released in 1977, it was a remarkable success, attracting in La Paz alone, a city of 750,000 inhabitants, between 200,000 and 250,000 spectators. This is an outstanding record, not only for local films but also vis-a-vis imported films.[11] Insofar as the 120 Bolivian theatres are located mostly in the main cities and towns, (30 of these theatres are in La Paz), Eguino's films were geared more to the middle classes, students, and intellectuals that attend these theatres and not to a then unreachable peasant audience.

Attempts at Commercial Filmmaking

Few feature films have been made in Bolivia besides the ones produced by the Ukamau group. Beginning in the early 1960s the country saw the emer-

---

[11] This success clearly confirms what this book has noted for all the other countries studied: Latin American spectators are really interested in seeing themselves on the screen in non-banal situations, and censorship and the other factors which have been described prevent them from this.

gence of two lines of filmmaking: a. films directed to a marginalized audience with consciousness-raising purposes, and b. films directed to urban audiences with principally commercial purposes. The films produced by the Ukamau group in its first phase were clearly within the bounds of the first approach. This line of filmmaking attempted through the medium of film what other intellectuals and writers had attempted through literary means. The written word (written in Spanish), however, implied a wider gap between intellectuals and Indian and peasant masses because of illiteracy and linguistic and cultural differences. It is not difficult to see that an attempt to reach peasant and Indian communities with critical messages in a medium that does not require literacy and in their own language, will meet censorship and other forms of repression from governments unsympathetic to radical social change.

On the other hand, in a small-market Latin American country, the approach to filmmaking that aims at reaching the urban audiences with films of wide commercial appeal will find the domestic market completely dominated, not only by U.S. and some European films, but also by the products of the larger Latin American countries. In most cases such a domestic market will be insufficient to recoup investments, and this difficulty will be compounded by the absence of any significant exterior market, not even the limited markets of other Latin American countries.

It is not surprising then that few commercially oriented films have been made in Bolivia, and that most of these films have insisted on *folklorismo* as a strategy to emphasize inocuous local aspects and increase the domestic market appeal. A large proportion of Latin American intellectuals regard *folklorismo* as a false view of folklore and society, a superficial view of folkloric expressions devoid of their social and historical context.

Detrás de los Andes (Beyond the Andes, 1952, unfinished) was the first attempt at commercial sound feature film in Bolivia. The optimism and momentum brought about by the 1952 nationalist revolution fueled the belief that the new political project would open new avenues for private enterprise in all areas of the Bolivian economy. This film was left unfinished due to the lack of sufficient financial resources, and no other such ventures were attempted until the late 1960s.

Released by Ruiz in 1969, *Mina Alaska* (Alaska Mine) was an attempt to make a film of wide commercial appeal. This film incorporated a good amount of footage from *Detrás de los Andes,* and had some success in La Paz and other cities of the interior. In 1969 and 1970, Bolivia saw renewed activity in commercial filmmaking, centered now on co-productions as an attempt to garner better financial resources and a larger market. Two co-productions were made in 1969, one with Spain and the other with Argentina and Chile. One co-production with Argentina was made in 1970. The above attempts were not fruitful, and have not been repeated.

Two features can be counted in the line of commercial filmmaking in the period of the Banzer government (1971–1978).[12] In 1976 a new production company, Sudameris Films, produced *La Chaskanawi* (Starry-Eyed Indian Girl), a film version of a famous 1940s Bolivian novel written by Carlos Medinacelli. Although the original novel for the 1976 film was clear in its denunciation of a strongly prejudiced and even racist society, the film presented a very superficial view of social problems, emphasizing instead the more "colorful" folkloric aspects of the story. Directed by the brothers Cuellar (who produced and directed *El Celibato* (Celibacy) in 1979), the film enjoyed a public but not a critical success.

The second film was *El Embrujo de mi Tierra* (Bewitching Land), finished by the end of 1977 and directed by Jorge Guerra. This film included a very lightly knitted story woven to lend unity to a superficial folkloric revue.

In July 1978, the political arena saw a presidential election remarkable for the massive-scale fraud in favor of Banzer's chosen successor, Gen. Pereda. Despite his sponsor's expectations, and in a context of mobilization of trade unions, students, and other opposition groups, the official candidate seized power and proclaimed a government of "democratic transition." Pereda initiated a process of dismantling Banzer's repressive system, a process that gained further momentum when Gen. Padilla assumed the presidency. It was under the above conditions that it was possible to give limited distribution to the films that Sanjinés had made in exile. These films, however, were shown in trade unions and in a brief cycle at the Cinemateca (Film Society) but not in commercial theatres. The government ordered the cycle discontinued.

Against a background of renewed political instability, widespread calls for democratization and intermittent but cruel repression, (for instance, under the government of Gen. García Meza, July 1980 to August 1981), perpsectives for the emergence of new modes of filmmaking in Bolivia have switched to the University, trade unions, film societies, and other social and political movements.[13] Between 1978 and 1981, the most

[12] Bolivian film critic Mesa Gisbert (1979, p. 35) has judged this approach rather harshly, as an approach to filmmaking that turned its back to the reality of Latin American film, ignored a reality made of wide social inequalities, and did not have the technical and/or financial means to make films with an acceptable standard of quality that might be profitable beyond the national borders. Mesa Gisbert added: "In Bolivia, this type of film attempts to forget, by means of a *folklorista* and *costumbrista* surface, the real life lived by the various social strata and racial groups" (1979, p. 61).

[13] Keen and Wasserman (1980, p. 381) stated: "In the violent ebb and flow of Bolivia politics since 1964, governments have risen and fallen, but a persistent theme has been the conflict between radical workers, students, and nationalist military, on the one hand, and a coalition uniting remnants of the old landowning aristocracy, a new elite of businessmen and politicians grown wealthy through U.S. aid, and conservative military, on the other."

dynamic aspect of Bolivian filmmaking has been the momentum gained by a movement to make films in super-8 format. This movement is supported by trade unions, student groups, and universities.

CONCLUDING REMARKS

This chapter provides, through the case of Bolivia, a historically situated overview of the conditions faced by local filmmaking in small-market Latin American countries. Despite remarkable differences in historical development, social structure, and ethnic composition, a relatively similar situation for local filmmaking could have been described for Ecuador, Paraguay, Uruguay, or the Central American nations.

The specific case of Bolivia makes it possible to observe filmmaking under conditions of complete absence of state protection for private production (as opposed to government-sponsored production), marked delay in the introduction of relevant technologies, and the extreme scarcity of technical infrastructure for feature film production. As an example, it can be mentioned that no facilities for 35mm film development, printing, and editing, exist in Bolivia today (1982). (Bolivian television only has facilities for developing and editing 16mm film.) Bolivian feature films are usually processed in Argentina, Brazil, or the U.S.

The evolution of the Bolivian Film Institute and its eventual dissolution in the late 1960s has also made it possible to see the difficulties of the government of a capitalist dependent country to maintain ideological control of filmmaking under conditions of protracted social conflict, and how it has preferred to concentrate such resources and control in the new mass medium, television.

Chapter 8
Latin American Cinema: The Uncertain Screen

The Hollywood film has accustomed us to expect a narrative form that has definite closure, either a happy or a tragic ending. In real life, however, closure of ongoing processes will always seem arbitrary. Film production, distribution, exhibition, and consumption in Latin America are open processes, complex activities still unfolding. Depending upon domestic contexts, foreign markets, and government policies, these activities might still find new forms of articulation with television, the thriving and relatively new video-cassette market, smaller film formats, and other technologies. Film as a medium could maintain greater freedom of experimentation than other mass media, but this will not happen under the forces of the market alone, even less if the market is only the remnant of what multinational distributors have occupied. Such a vision seems to require communication policies and participatory planning going well beyond state protection for national entrepreneurs.

Chapter 1 began by distinguishing a set of variables and social agencies that have affected the growth perspectives of Latin American film industries and the content of their productions. The cases studied in the subsequent chapters gave specificity to the above aspects, and made apparent the difficulty of generalizing across the variety of national experiences. Instead of attempting an impossible closure, this chapter will offer some general reflections suggested by the case studies presented in the previous chapters, concentrating mostly on problems of state policy towards local cinematographies.

In recent years, the debate over the degree of freedom of or restraint on mass media products and other messages crossing national borders has been one of the focal points of discussion in the policymaking and policy research forums concerned with international communications (Gunter, 1978; Nordenstreng and Schiller, 1979).

"Free flow" advocates contend that the unhindered circulation of messages among nations will result in equal benefits for all the parties involved. Although this may become true in some cases, and there is no doubt that developing countries might benefit from a freer access to oftentimes proprietary scientific and technical information, ideas and culture are also material forces, embedded in cultural products that in market-oriented societies are expected to derive profits from their production and circulation. From this perspective, critics of the free flow position assert that when the cultural products of advanced countries massively dominate developing markets, not only the possibility of any major growth of local production is preempted, but a standard is set for the use of the imported communication technologies. Moreover, such standards and models of mass media use may not be the most adequate to developing countries' national integration and the developmental needs of the majority of their populations.

Although no attempt has been made to cover the above debate in detail, the preceding chapters are better comprehended when projected against the general background of such discussions. It is then in the spirit of studying the past in order to derive useful insights into current and future policy issues that the present study was conducted. Even though film is by no means a new technology, and its economic and ideological importance as the foremost audio-visual mass medium has been reduced by the widespread diffusion of television, many of the problems and dilemmas surrounding the introduction of new communication technologies in developing countries can already be seen operating in the case of feature films, suggesting that the problem of cultural dependence is not a new one, but one perhaps made more acute by the advent of satellites and the wide array of new communication technologies.

From our overview of state policies and local filmmaking in Argentina, Mexico, Brazil, Chile, and Bolivia, a picture emerges of the main forces affecting the development of Latin American cinemas. The main social forces in this process were (and continue to be): 1. foreign capitalists (mostly U.S.-based distributors) that in some cases own some showcase theatres; national capitalists, that sharply divide into 2. producers or producer-directors and 3. exhibitors; 4. professional groups (actors, technicians, film industry workers, etc.); 5. the state; and 6. the audiences.

Film industries in Latin America developed within an international context of oligopolic control of production, technology, raw material (film stock), and distribution channels. As Chapter 2 has shown, film as business adopted a global perspective from its very beginnings. Latin American film production developed in domestic markets created on the basis of the products of the advanced capitalist countries, and local entrepreneurs had to approach filmmaking as an import-substitution process. Many of these entrepreneurs began as producers, distributors, and exhibitors, but later (especially after World War I) specialized as distributors or exhibitors, dependent upon foreign productions, but enjoying commercial stability.

While producers and producer-directors had a stake in the industrial aspects of filmmaking, and were consequently interested in the expansion of the domestic market and in the continuity of local production, exhibitors were mostly interested in the commercial aspects of the activity, and depended on foreign distributors (producers also depended on foreign suppliers of technology, film etc). The state acted (and continues to act) as mediator among all these groups, favoring one or the other according to the orientation of the various governments. The case of state protection for Brazilian films in the 1970s (Chapter 5) also indicates that under certain conditions the state may become the sponsor of cultural productions not necessarily appealing to a mass market, although an international market might be thought to be the target in this case. An alternative view would see this as prestige production, in the same fashion as in the era of the studio system in Hollywood when some films were made as a prestige enterprise subsidized by other more commercial productions.

For all Latin American film industries, the massive presence of foreign productions has always been a basic determining factor. This has not only been the result of impersonal market forces but active promotion by some sectors of the activity, forcing local film producers and directors to compete through a constant dialectic of imitation or differentiation from imported productions.[1]

Perhaps one of the most profound effects on developing countries cultural creativity has been the incorporation, not only of technologies, but also cultural forms and modes of use of the new media that, in the case of film, involved the importation of a defined manner of institutional organization. All Latin American film industries, even the smallest, began by attempting to imitate the Hollywood studio, a form of organization embedded in the dominant technology itself. Only the advent and diffusion of lighter technical equipment (also originated in advanced capitalist countries) and non-studio forms of filmmaking allowed going beyond the Hollywood model. The rejection of this model in Latin America involved complex generational and politico-ideological issues, coupled in some cases with radically different intended audiences and an alternative overall mode of use of the medium (see *Tiers Monde*, 1979, pp. 615–645). If the "auteur" theory of filmmaking can be seen as the first step beyond the dominant

---

[1] It is within this frame that *folklorismo* seems to have functioned as an important early device for the "localization" of film content.

model of filmmaking, collective film production, alternative distribution, and audience activation and discussion, as undertaken in several Latin American countries, has been a further step in the same direction.

Whenever the organization of film production in Latin America (and this is more apparent in smaller markets) attempted to replicate Hollywood style studio setups, this approach disregarded the fact that Hollywood studios were based on incomparably larger domestic and international markets, and were the product of an earlier vertical integration. This earlier vertical integration allowed U.S. companies to enter the oligopolic sector of the economy in its own country and in many foreign markets, while in most cases Latin American film production and distribution remained in the competitive sectors of their own economies. The sustained and continuous access to foreign markets was a basic element in the growth of the U.S. film industry, as it was and continues to be a basic aspect of the success of the Mexican film industry, that can also count on the large Latino population in the U.S., perhaps the only growing market for Spanish-speaking films in the 1980s.[2]

In terms of market size, it is interesting to note that the growth problems encountered by the national film industries in large countries like Argentina, Brazil, and Mexico, were replicated at a different level in smaller countries. In Chile, for instance, while the massive presence of U.S. distributors took over a sizeable part of the audience, the sector of the audience preferring Spanish-speaking films found a steady supply of Argentine and Mexican productions. Chilean filmmakers difficulties were thus compounded. In terms of mass communication policies and planning, this type of relation among countries in the periphery of capitalism suggests a complex agenda for future consideration.

In each Latin American country, local film production developed not only according to its domestic and international market but also in accordance with the importance and limits that the ruling groups assigned to it as part of the ideological state apparatuses.[3] In some cases, it has been possible for local filmmakers to make films incorporating a critical view of local reality. Sometimes this was done within the framework of the estab-

[2] The U.S. is the fastest growing market in the Latin world, with about 15,000,000 legal residents, a total estimated at 25,000,000, and 650 theatres. Most of the films for this market come from Mexico, with occasional films from Spain, Argentina, or Colombia. Countrywide billings have been estimated to reach $20,000,000. The more important distributors are Azteca Films (Mexican, state owned) and Televicine (Mexican, private, affiliated with Televisa). (Variety, March 17, 1982, pp. 48; 82) This might be a relatively short term market, however, as future growth might be limited by youth assimilation (Variety, March 17, 1982, pp.49; 80.

[3] Although it cannot be elaborated here, this type of consideration brings to the fore the problem of the typical features of the state in capitalist dependent countries, and the typical forms in which ideological state apparatuses have been organized. This last aspect has been referred to by Cesareo (1979) as "the form of the apparatus."

lished mode of film production, distribution, and consumption. In several recent cases, it has been done outside the above framework. The attempts at alternative filmmaking in Chile and Bolivia (presented in Chapters 6 and 7) made apparent not only the specific difficulties faced by local film-making in small and intermediate market Latin American countries, but also that a rejection of the dominant form of cinema may entail not only a different mode of production but also alternative modes of distribution and consumption (popular assemblies, discussion groups, etc.).[4]

STATE PROTECTION

In order to counteract the power of foreign distributors and their (more or less antagonistic) alliance with local exhibitors, the most obvious response has been the design and implementation of state protectionist policies. Generally speaking, the need for state protectionism for mass media industries can be predicated on the basis of three main arguments: economic, political, and cultural. According to the economic argument, state protection for local mass media industries is necessary as part of a set of measures designed to curb imports and reduce either the drain in the foreign currency reserve or the debt of the country in question. The political argument stresses the actual or potential role of mass media as part of a system supporting developmental efforts and/or contributing to national identity and integration. This leads to the cultural argument, according to which local mass media industries are necessary to preserve the cultural heritage and integrity of the various nations and peoples of the world. Perhaps a fourth argument might be added, a professional argument affirming the need to protect local mass media industries in order to maintain a pool of highly skilled mass communications technicians in every country.

On the basis of any combination of the above justifications, state protectionism for local production can be seen as a basic ingredient of national communication policies in developing countries. Different combinations of protectionist measures will certainly yield different quantitative and cultural results, but the choice and implementation of protectionist measures for local mass media industries is not a simple task, and is not made easier by the fact that diverse pressure groups espouse widely different views on the matter. The cases studied in this book indicate that the final effects of protectionist measures will depend not only on their design and implementation but also on their interaction with other significant elements in the domestic and international contexts of the societies in question.

[4] The problem of how to go beyond commercial exhibition circuits without necessarily rejecting these circuits has been a recurrent theme for critical Latin American filmmakers.

The analyses in the preceding chapters highlighted the importance of state protectionism for the survival and growth of mass communication industries in developing countries. Such survival and growth can be thought of as a necessary but not sufficient condition for the eventual social utilization of mass communications (as distinct from use dictated only by the profit motive). The question then arises about the most effective forms of state support for local mass media industries. In the case of film, a helpful distinction (presented in Chapter 4) can be made between restrictive and supportive protectionism. A purely *restrictive* state protectionist policy would concentrate on measures designed to impede a complete takeover of the domestic film market by foreign products (by means of screen quotas, import quotas, high import taxes, etc.). A *supportive* state protectionist policy would concentrate on different forms of assistance to the local film industry (bank loans, production subsidies, organization of a foreign distribution service for local films, scholarships and fellowships for local technicians, etc.). A *comprehensive* state protectionist policy would include both restrictive (of foreign competition) and supportive (of local production) aspects. The cases studied in the present book, however, made apparent that perhaps the most important aspect of protectionism is the political will to support national film production more than the technocratic problem of the best specific measures.

A carefully designed and implemented protectionist policy can certainly promote the *growth* of local mass media industries. The notion of *development,* however, encompasses qualitative as well as quantitative concerns, or at least a view of the communication process not solely in terms of production but also in terms of distribution and audience use. These factors could be accommodated by comprehensive communication policies that presuppose the planning of other social aspects of mass communication besides protectionism. Ideally, such aspects would be better contemplated by participatory rather than by authoritarian forms of planning.

CENSORSHIP

Statements by defenders of the "free flow of communication" point of view (i.e., Pool, 1979, p. 140) tend to confuse state protection of local mass media production with government censorship, arguing that state protection will ultimately become government censorship of mass media content. Our study of Latin American cinematographies, however, makes apparent that protectionism and censorship are relatively differentiated state functions. In fact, in all the countries studied in the present book it is possible to point out instances of films made with state support and then questioned or banned by censorship. Although state-organized and en-forced, it should not be forgotten that in many cases some forms of film censorship in Latin America are demanded and supported by influential social and religious groups.

In all Latin American countries censorship predated by decades the design and implementation of any form of protectionism. Even today, smaller Latin American countries that do not have any protectionist sys-tem for local production in operation have efficient censorship systems. For dominant groups in society, censorship is one more area of exercise of their ideological hegemony. All films, foreign and domestic, are reviewed by censorship boards, although in many cases local films receive more careful scrutiny. This might be explained by the fact that, for a variety of reasons discussed throughout this book, local films appeal predominantly to popular audiences, and familiar locales might increase identification and the subsequent ideological effect.[5]

The state has a much wider ideological role than that of censor; it not only guarantees the reproduction of the dominant mode of production in film (and in society as a whole), but also (and perhaps even more impor-tant) the mode of distribution and the mode of "appropriate" consumption of films, the medium's mode of utilization. Recognizing that the dominant conditions of message reception (the message pragmatic aspects) may par-tially neutralize messages' semantic content, the state attempts to control not only message content (through censorship) but also the conditions of message reception.[6]

Ideally, the communication components of peoples' developmental efforts would be better accommodated by a combination of unobtrusive state protection and complete freedom of expression. This utopia, how-ever, will always have to be negotiated by filmmakers and other interested groups in the concrete socio-economic and political conditions obtaining in each country. In the same fashion as the overall social order in society is not imposed once and forever, but is constantly negotiated, produced, and reproduced, cultural producers will have to struggle for wider participa-tion in the establishment of the conditions of production, circulation, and consumption of their products.

[5] Censorship is a politico-ideological instrument with wider implications than the ones affecting films. For instance, in Brazil in the early 1970s not only films were subject to cen-sorship but also newspapers, magazines, radio and television, books, and even paintings (Weil et al., 1975, Chapters 8 and 11).

[6] The dominant commercial mode of use does not allow either time or space for post-view-ing discussion of film content among spectators. Critical filmmakers that questioned not only film content but attempted to implement alternative modes of utilization outside the-atre settings and to encourage popular debate of film content have been the most perse-cuted in Latin America. For convincing evidence of repressive governmental practices against films and filmmakers in Latin America see the collective volume *America Latina: Lo Schermo Contesso*, Venice: Marsilio, 1981.

The case of Latin American films suggests that some form of state protection seems unavoidable if local film production is to maintain presence and continuity. Protectionism, the struggle for freedom of expression, and participatory communications planning will only find integration and coherence through the formulation, open discussion, and implementation of explicit national and international communication policies.

Appendix
Statistical Tables

Table 1
Market Size Indicators for Theatrical Motion Pictures
in Selected Latin American Countries, 1934 and 1981

	Population (1934) (000)	Theatres (1934)	Population (1980, est.) (000)	Theatres (1978)	Annual Attendance (1981) (000)	Attendance per Capita (1981)
Argentina	18,835	1,985	27,064	1,004	65,600	2.5
Brazil	40,272	1,125	123,032	2,973	208,300	1.8
Mexico	16,527	701	71,911	2,400	262,400	4.1
Chile	—	180	11,104	231	19,400	1.8
Colombia	7,851	385	27,520	682	96,000	4.0
Peru	6,237	100	17,780	338	—	—
Venezuela	3,250	134	13,913	577	33,000	2.6
Bolivia	3,014	25	5,600	200	3,200	0.9
Ecuador	2,500	22	8,354	185	38,700	5.6

Sources: Population and No. Theatres, 1934: *Variety,* 11/6/1934 (Chile: *Variety,* 5/19/1937).
Population 1980 (est.): *United Nations Demographic Yearbook 1980.*
Theatres (1978): *Unesco Statistical Yearbook 1981.*
Annual Cinema Attendance, Total and Per Capita, 1981: *Encyclopedia Britannica 1982 Book of the Year.*

Table 2
Chilean Feature Films Released in the Silent Era, 1916–1931

Year	No. of Films	Year	No. of Films
1916	1	1924	10
1917	3	1925	16
1918	2	1926	18
1919	2	1927	4
1920	4	1928	2
1921	4	1929	3
1922	3	1930	1
1923	6	1931	1
		TOTAL	80

Source: Compiled by the author from data in Godoy Quezada (1966).

Table 3
National Film Production in Argentina, Bolivia, Brazil, Chile, and Mexico, 1930–1981

Year	Argentina (Releases)	Mexico (Production)	Brazil (Production)	Chile (Releases)	Bolivia (Releases)
1930		1	18		
1931	4	1	17		
1932	2	4	14		
1933	6	12	10		
1934	6	25	7	1	
1935	13	26	6		
1936	15	25	7		
1937	28	38	6		
1938	41	57	8		1
1939	50	37	7	5	

116

continued

Table 3 (Continued)

Year	Argentina (Releases)	Mexico (Production)	Brazil (Production)	Chile (Releases)	Bolivia (Releases)
1940	49	27	13	4	
1941	47	46	4		
1942	56	49	4	5	
1943	36	67	8	3	
1944	24	78	9	5	
1945	23	79	8	6	
1946	32	74	10	8	
1947	38	53	11	7	
1948	41	81	15	3	
1949	47	108	21	3	
1950	56	124	20	2	
1951	53	103	22	3	
1952	35	99	34	2	
1953	37	76	29		
1954	45	105	25	2	
1955	43	90	28	1	
1956	36	91	29	1	
1957	15	92	36	1	
1958	32	104	44		1
1959	22	84	34	1	
1960	31	89	34	1	
1961	25	48	30	1	
1962	32	55	27	2	
1963	27	42	32		
1964	37	67	27	1	
1965	30	80*	33	1	
1966	34	80*	28		1
1967	25	80*	44	4	
1968	40	80*	54	5	
1969	31	80*	53	5	2
1970	33	80*	83	4	
1971	34	75	94	3	
1972	32	64	70	3	
1973	39	52	58	6	
1974	39	50	77	1	1
1975	33	43	85		
1976	20	42	84		1
1977	21	68	73		1
1978	22	66	101		1
1979	31	85	93	1	
1980	34	90	102		
1981	24	65	80		

Sources: Argentina: *Heraldo del Cine* 1/4/1967; Instituto Nacional de Cinematografia, *Memoria 1973; International Motion Picture Almanac;* Martin (1977, 1978, 1979); *Variety.* Mexico: Sadoul (1954); Garcia Riera (1969); Heuer (1964); *International Motion Picture Almanac; International Film Guide; Variety.* Brazil: Embrafilme (quoted in P aranagua, 1981); *Variety* 3/17/82, p. 65. Chile: Godoy Quezada (1966); Ossa Coo (1971); Chanan (1976); *Variety.* Bolivia: Mesa Gisbert (1976, 1979); Gumucio Dragon (1981).

Note: * denotes average 1965–1971.

Table 4
Films Released in Argentina from 6/1/1931 to 12/31/1931, by Distributor

Distributor	Number of Films	Percent (N = 244)
1. Larger U.S. Companies		
Paramount	42	17.2%
Metro	36	14.7%
Warner	25	10.2%
Fox	20	8.1%
Columbia	16	6.5%
Universal	7	2.8%
United Artists	6	2.4%
Subtotal	152	62.2%
2. European Companies		
Terra	13	5.3%
Filmreich	7	2.8%
Gaumont British	6	2.4%
Subtotal	26	10.5%
3. Glucksman	22	9.0%
4. Others*	44	18.0%
Totals	244	100.0%

Source: Computed from data in *Heraldo del cine,* 1931
* The category "Others" in Table 4 includes local distributors of U.S. and European films not distributed by the larger companies, and might include some European distributors not detected by the data collection procedure.

Table 5

Films Released in Argentina in 1935, by Distributor

Distributor	Number of Films	Percent (N = 504)
1. Larger U.S. Companies		
Paramount	63	12.5%
Metro	40	7.9%
Warner	45	8.9%
Fox	54	10.7%
Columbia	40	7.9%
Universal	44	8.7%
United Artists	22	4.3%
RKO	47	9.3%
Subtotal	355	70.4%
2. Smaller U.S. Companies		
Liberty	23	4.5%
Monograph	9	1.7%
Subtotal	32	6.2%
3. European Companies		
Gaumont British	17	3.3%
UFA	19	3.7%
Other European	17	3.3%
Subtotal	53	10.5%
4. Other Distributors	42	10.3%
5. Argentine Productions	13	2.5%
Totals	504	100.0%

Source: Adapted from Bruski (1936).

Table 6
Films Released in Argentina in 1950, by Distributor

Distributor	Number of Films	Percent (N = 187)
1. Larger U.S. Companies		
Paramount	4	2.1%
Metro	0	0.0%
Warner	1	0.0%
Fox	7	3.7%
Columbia	9	4.8%
Universal	0	0.0%
United Artists	19	10.1%
RKO	2	1.0%
Subtotal	42	22.4%
2. Smaller U.S. Companies		
Republic	3	1.6%
3. Argentine Productions	56	29.9%
4. Other	86	45.9%
Totals	187	100.0%

Source: Computed from data in Heraldo del Cine, 1950.

Table 7
Films Released in Argentina in 1954, by Distributor

Distributor	Number of Films	Percent (N = 368)
1. Larger U.S. Companies		
Paramount	23	6.2%
Metro	30	8.1%
Warner	30	8.1%
Fox	20	5.4%
Columbia	34	9.2%
Universal	25	6.7%
United Artists	23	6.2%
RKO	29	7.8%
Subtotal	214	58.1%
2. Smaller U.S. Companies		
Republic	20	5.4%
Allied Artists	13	3.5%
Subtotal	33	8.9%
3. Argentine Productions	45	12.2%
4. Other	76	20.6%
Totals	368	100.0%

Source: Computed from data in Heraldo del Cine, 1/12/1955.

Table 8
Films Released in Argentina in 1954, by Country of Origin

Country of Origin	Number of Films	Percent (N = 368)
Argentina	45	12.2%
United States	234	63.5%
Spain	24	6.5%
United Kingdom	17	4.6%
Italy	17	4.6%
France	12	3.2%
U.S.S.R.	8	2.1%
Other	11	2.9%
Totals	368	100.0%

Source: Heraldo del Cine, 1/12/1955.

Table 9
Screen Quota for National Films in Brazil, 1932–1981

Year	Screen Quota
1932	100 meters with each foreign film
1939	1 feature film/theatre/year
1946	3 feature film/theatre/year
1951	1 Brazilian film for 8 foreign films
1959	42 days/theatre/year
1963	56 days/theatre/year
1970	112 days/theatre/year
1970	98 days/theatre/year (exhibitors protest)
1972	84 days/theatre/year
1975	112 days/theatre/year (Embrafilme reorganized)
1978	133 days/theatre/year
1979	140 days/theatre/year

Source: Compiled by the author.

Table 10

Chilean Feature Films Released, by Government Period, 1932–1980

Government	Years	No. of Films
Alessandri (Liberal)	1932–1938	1
Aguirre Cerdá (*Radicalismo*)	1938–1942	14
Juan A. Ríos (*Radicalismo*)	1942–1946	22
Gonzalez Videla (*Radicalismo*)	1946–1952	20
Ibañez (Independent)	1952–1958	5
Alessandri (Right-wing Independent)	1958–1964	6
Frei (Christian Democrat)	1964–1970	19
Allende (Socialist)	1970–1973	12
Pinochet (Military Junta)	1973–	2

Sources: Computed from data in Godoy Quezada (1966), Ossa Coo (1971), Chanan (1976), *Variety.*

References

Aguilar, A., and Carmona, F. (1967). "Mexico: Riqueza y Miseria." Nuestro Tiempo, Mexico City.

Althusser, L. (1971). "Lenin and Philosophy." Monthly Review Press, New York.

"America Latina: Lo Schermo Contesso." (1981). Marsilio, Venice.

Anderson, B., and Cockcroft, J. (1972). Control and Cooptation in Mexican Politics. In Cockcroft, J., Gunder Frank A., and Johnson, D. (1972). "Dependence and Underdevelopment." Doubleday, New York.

Andrade, J. B. (1980). Estado e Cinema Brasileiro. In "Cineclub Debate Cultura." Conselho Nacional de Cineclub, São Paulo.

Balio, T. ed. (1976). "The American Film Industry." University of Wisconsin Press, Madison.

Bannock, G., Baxter, R., and Rees, R. (1977). "The Penguin Dictionary of Economics." Viking, New York.

Barnouw, E., and Krishnaswamy, S. (1980). "Indian Film." 2nd ed. Oxford University Press, New York.

Bernardet, J. C. (1979). "Cinema Brasileiro: Propostas para uma Historia." Paz e Terra, Rio de Janeiro.

Bolzoni, F. (1974). "El Cine de Allende." Torres, Valencia.

Boron, A. (1981). State forms in Latin America. New Left Review 130, 45–66.

Bruski, N. (1936). Activity in the Argentine. In "International Motion Picture Almanac 1936–1937." Quigley, New York.

Burns, E. B. (1980). "A History of Brazil." 2nd ed. Columbia University Press, New York.

Burton, J. (1978). The camera as "gun": Two decades of culture and resistance in Latin America. Latin American Perspectives 5, No. 1, 49–76.

Cardoso, F. H. (1977). The consumption of dependency theory in the United States. Latin American Research Review 12, 7–24.

Cardoso, F. H., and Faletto, E. (1979). "Dependency and Development in Latin America." University of California Press, Berkeley.

Cavalcanti, A. (1977). "Filme e Realidade." Artenova, Rio de Janeiro.

Cavarozzi, M., and Petras, J. (1974). Chile. *In* Chilcote, R. and Edelstein, J. (1974).

Cesareo, G. (1979). The 'form of the apparatus' in the mass media. *Media Culture and Society 1,* No. 3, 277-287.

Chanan, M. (1976). "Chilean Cinema." British Film Institute, London.

Chanan, M. (1980). Labour power and aesthetic labour in film and television in Britain. *Media, Culture and Society 2,* No. 2, 117-137.

Chilcote, R. and Edelstein, J., eds. (1974). "Latin America: The Struggle with Dependency and Beyond." Wiley, New York.

Ciria, A. (1974). Peronism yesterday and today. *Latin American Perspectives 1,* No. 3, 21-41.

Cockcroft, J. (1974). Mexico. *In* Chilcote and Edelstein, eds. (1974).

Cockcroft, J., Gunder Frank, A., and Johnson, D. (1972). "Dependence and Underdevelopment: Latin America's Political Economy." Doubleday, New York.

Collier, D., ed. (1979). "The New Authoritarianism in Latin America." Princeton University Press, Princeton, New Jersey.

Conant, J. (1960). "Antitrust in the Motion Picture Industry." University of California Press, Berkeley.

Conselho Nacional de Cineclub (1980). "Cineclub Debate Cultura", São Paulo.

Corradi, J. E. (1974). Argentina. *In* Chilcote and Edelstein, eds. (1974).

Daniels, E. (1970). From mercantilism to imperialism: The Argentine case. *Nacla Newsletter,* July–August 1970 (part 1); *Nacla Newsletter,* October 1970 (part 2).

Diccionario Porrua. (1964). Porrua, Mexico City.

Di Nubila, D. (1959-60). "Historia del Cine Argentino," 2 vols. Cruz de Malta, Buenos Aires.

Dos Santos, T. (1974). Brazil. *In* Chilcote and Edelstein, eds. (1974).

Ehrmann, H. (1973). Chile won't pay, US won't play. *Variety,* 3/1/1973, also in Chanan, M. (1976).

Encyclopedia Britannica. 15th edition, 1979, Chicago.

Evans, P. (1979). "Dependent Development: The Alliance of Multinational, State, and Local Capital in Brazil." Princeton University Press, Princeton, New Jersey.

Fagen, P. (1974). The media in Allende's Chile: Some contradictions. *Journal of Communication 24,* No. 1, 59-70.

Farias, R. (1982). Towards a Common Market of Portuguese and Spanish Speaking Countries. *In* Johnson, R. and Stam, R., eds. (1982).

Fejes, F. (1981). Media imperialism: an assessment. *Media, Culture and Society 3,* No. 3, 81-89.

Film Daily Yearbook of Motion Pictures. Published 1922-1970. The Film Daily Press, New York.

Fortune, Dec. 1938, pp. 69-72.

French, P. (1971). "The Movie Moguls." Penguin, London.

Galvao, M. R. (1982). Vera Cruz: A Brazilian Hollywood. *In* Johnson, R. and Stam, R., eds. (1982).

Garcia Riera, E. (1969-78). "Historia Documental del Cine Mexicano," 9 vols. Era, Mexico City.

Garcia Riera, E. (1981). Mexique. *In* Hennebelle, G. and Gumucio-Dragon, A., eds. (1981).

Godoy Quezada, M. (1966). "Historia del Cine Chileno." Santiago de Chile.

Goffman, E. (1974). "Frame Analysis." University of Pennsylvania Press, Philadelphia.

Gonzaga, A., and Salles Gomes, P. E. (1966). "70 Anos de Cinema Brasileiro." Expressão y Cultura, Rio de Janeiro.

Gordon, D. (1976). Why the Movie Majors are Major. *In* Balio, T., ed. (1976).

Guback, T. (1969). "The International Film Industry." Indiana University Press, Bloomington.

Guback, T. (1976). Hollywood's International Market. *In* Balio, T., ed. (1976).

Guback, T. (1979). Theatrical Film. *In* Compaine, B., ed. "Who Owns the Media?" Harmony, New York.

Gumucio Dragon, A. Bolivie. *In* Hennebelle, G. and Gumucio Dragon, A., eds. (1981).

Gunter, J. (1978). An introduction to the great debate. *Journal of Communication 28,* No. 4, 142–156.

Hamilton, N. (1982). "The Limits of State Autonomy: Post-Revolutionary Mexico." Princeton University Press, Princeton.

Hennebelle, G. and Gumucio Dragón, A., eds. (1981). "Les Cinemas de L'Amerique Latine." L'Herminier, Paris.

Hennessy, A. (1968). Bolivia. *In* Veliz, C., ed. "Latin America and the Caribbean, a Handbook." Praeger, New York.

Heraldo del Cine, Buenos Aires, March 1, 1944.

Heraldo del Cine, Buenos Aires, Jan. 12, 1955.

Heraldo del Cine, Buenos Aires, May 11, 1955.

Heraldo del Cine, Buenos Aires, Nov. 2, 1955.

Heraldo del Cine, Buenos Aires, Jan. 4, 1967.

Heuer, F. (1964). "La Industria Cinematográfica Mexicana." Mexico City.

Huettig, M. (1944). "Economic Control of the Motion Picture Industry." University of Pennsylvania Press, Philadelphia.

Ianni, O. (1978). O estado e a organizacao da cultura. *In Encontros com a Civilizacao Brasileira* No. 1, Rio de Janeiro, July 1978.

"International Film Guide." Published yearly beginning in 1968. Tantivity Press, London.

"International Motion Picture Almanac." 1930–1980. Quigley Publishing Co., New York.

Jobes, H. (1966). "Motion Pictures Empire." Archon Books, Hamden.

Johnson, R. (1982a). State Policy Toward the Film Industry in Brazil. Presented at the Convention of the Latin American Studies Association, Washington, D.C., March 5, 1982.

Johnson, R. (1982b). State Policy toward the Film Industry in Brazil. Technical Paper No. 36. Available from the Institute of Latin American Studies, The University of Texas at Austin.

Johnson, R., and Stam, R., eds. (1982). "Brazilian Cinema." Fairleigh Dickinson University Press, Rutherford, NJ.

Keen, B., and Wasserman, M. (1980). "A Short History of Latin America." Houghton Mifflin, Boston.

Klein, H. S. (1979). History of Bolivia. In Encyclopedia Britannica, 1979, Vol. 3, pp. 9–13.

Laclau, E. (1977). "Politics and Ideology in Marxist Theory." New Left Books, London.

Lopez, L. (1972). "Battle for better films in Chile's cinemas. *Morning Star.* 5/26/1972. (also in Chanan, M. ed., 1976).

Mahieu, A. (1974). "Breve Historia del Cine Nacional." Alzamor, Buenos Aires.

Martin, J. A. (1977). "Cine Argentino '76." Metrocop, Buenos Aires.

Martin, J. A. (1978). "Cine Argentino '77." Metrocop, Buenos Aires.

Martin, J. A. (1979). "Cine Argentino '78." Cero Seis, Buenos Aires.

Mesa Gisbert, C. (1976). "El Cine en Bolivia." Cinemateca de La Paz, La Paz, Bolivia.

Mesa Gisbert, C., ed. (1979). "Cine Boliviano: Del Realizador al Critico." Gisbert, La Paz, Bolivia.

Metz, C. (1975). The imaginary signifier. *Screen* 16, No. 2, 14–76.

Metz, C. (1979). The cinematic apparatus as social institution. *Discourse* No. 1, 7–37.

Montagu, I. (1968). "Film World." Penguin, London.

Mora, C. J. (1982). "Mexican Cinema: Reflections of a Society 1896–1980." University of California Press, Berkeley.

Nordenstreng, K., and Schiller, H., eds. (1979). "National Sovereignty and International Communication." Ablex, Norwood, NJ.

O'Donnell, G. (1973). "Modernization and Bureaucratic-Authoritarianism." Institute of

International Studies. University of California, Berkeley.

Ossa Coo, C. (1971). "Historia del Cine Chileno." Quimantu, Santiago de Chile.

Packenham, R. (1978). The New Utopianism: Political Development Ideas in the Dependency Literature. Working Paper No. 19, The Wilson Center, Smithsonian Institution, Washington, D.C.

Paranagua, P. A. (1981). Brésil. In Hennebelle, G. and Gumucio Dragon, A., eds. (1981).

Peralta Ramos, M. (1972). "Etapas de Acumulación y Alianzas de Clases en la Argentina 1930-1970." Siglo XXI, Buenos Aires.

Perez Turrent, T., and Turner, G. (1976). Mexico. In "International Film Guide 1977." Tantivity Press, London.

Perez Turrent, T., and Turner, G. (1979). Mexico. In "International Film Guide 1980." Tantivity Press, London.

Perez Turrent, T., and Turner, G. (1980). Mexico. In "International Film Guide 1981." Tantivity Press, London.

Phillips, J. (1975). Film Conglomerate "Blockbusters." Journal of Communication 25, No. 2, 171-182.

Pinto, A. (1973). Hollywood's Spanish-Language films. Films in Review 24, 473-485.

Pool, I. de S. (1979). Direct Broadcast Satellites and the Integrity of National Cultures. In Nordenstreng, K. and Schiller, H., eds. (1979).

Rabben, L. (1982). Opening Brazil to democracy?. Democracy 2, No. 3, 91-96.

Sadoul, G. (1947-1954). "Histoire Générale du Cinéma." 6 vols. Denoel, Paris. Vols. 1 and 2 (1947), vol. 3, part 1 (1951), part 2 (1952), vol. 6 (1954) [second ed., 1973].

Sadoul, G. (1964). "Louis Lumiere." Seghers, Paris.

Salles Gomes, P. E. (1982). Cinema: A Trajectory within Underdevelopment. In Johnson, R. and Stam, R., eds. (1982).

Sanchez, A. R. (1981). "Mitología de un Cine en Crisis." Premia, Mexico.

Sanjinés, J. (1979). "Teoría y Practica de un Cine Junto al Pueblo." Siglo XXI, Mexico.

Santos Pereira, G. (1973). "Plano Geral do Cinema Brasileiro." Borsoi, Rio de Janeiro.

Schnitman, J. A. (1979). "The Argentine Film Industry: A Contextual Study." Ph. D. Dissertation, Stanford University.

Schnitman, J. A. (1980). "State Protectionism and Film Industry Development: A Comparative View of Argentina and Mexico." Presented at the Conference of World Communications, The Annenberg School of Communications, University of Pennsylvania, April 1980.

Schnitman, J. A. (1981). Economic Protectionism and Mass Media Development: Film Industry in Argentina. In McAnany, G., Schnitman, J. A. and Janus, N., eds., "Communication and Social Structure: Critical Studies in Mass Media Research." Praeger, New York.

Scobie, J. (1971). "Argentina." Oxford University Press, New York.

Sweezy, P. (1956). "The Theory of Capitalist Development." Monthly Review Press, New York. (1st. ed., 1942).

Tabbia, A. (1979). Argentina. In "International Film Guide 1980." Tantivity Press, London.

Tiers Monde (1979). 20, No. 79, 615-645.

Torres, A., and Perez Estremera, M. (1973). "Nuevo Cine Latinoamericano." Anagrama, Barcelona.

Tunstall, J. (1977). "The Media are American." Columbia University Press, New York.

Turner, F. (1968). "The Dynamic of Mexican Nationalism." University of North Carolina Press, Chapel Hill.

Usabel, G. (1975). "American Films in Latin America: The Case History of United Artists Corporation 1919-1951." Ph.D. Dissertation, University of Wisconsin, Madison.

Variety, Feb. 26, 1936, p. 22. First Brazil film survey shows $8,000,000 annual biz, 80% to U.S. distribs; language not a problem.

Variety, Dec. 14, 1938, p. 17. Survey of Latin film market.

Variety, June 30, 1943, p. 25. Alstock talks of upping Mexican film facilities.

Variety, July 7, 1943, p. 19. U.S. still holding back on raw film stock to Argentina.

Variety, March 27, 1946, p. 21. Johnston stresses strong government aid to combat foreign snags to U.S. pix.

Variety, May 17, 1950, p. 12. State Dept. heeds Hollywood plea to help 'em abroad.

Variety, June 7, 1950, p. 15. Local pix crowd Argentine screens.

Variety, Oct. 10, 1956, p. 11. Un-united Americans sure to lose.

Variety, May 19, 1976, pp. 1; 126. Brazil eases up on tax, take-out.

Variety, March 25, 1981, pp. 75; 92. After N.Y. and Lisbon offices, Embrafilme to B.A. and Caracas.

Variety, March 17, 1982, pp. 48; 82. Latin film markets.

Variety, March 17, 1982, pp. 49; 80. Spanish market growth in U.S. limited by youth assimilation.

Vega, A. (1979). "Re-Vision del Cine Chileno." Aconcagua, Santiago de Chile.

Veliz, C., ed., (1968). "Latin America and the Caribbean, a Handbook." Praeger, New York.

Weil, T., Black, J. K., Blutstein, H., Hoyer, H., Johnston, K., and McMorris, D. (1974). "Area Handbook for Bolivia." The American University, Washington, DC

Weil, T., Black, J. K., Blutstein, H., Johnston, K., and McMorris, D. "Area Handbook for Brazil." The American University, Washington, DC

Name Index

Italic page numbers indicate complete bibliographic citations.

Subject Index